Software Solutions Corp

Understanding SQL Server 2005 - 2008 Tools and Technology

Introduction to SQL Server 2005 Supporting Technology – What you need to know to get started...

Credits and Acknowledgements:

Written by:	Rigoberto Garcia
Edited by:	Rigoberto Garcia and Karen Montalva
Cover Design by:	Karen Montalva
ISBN:	978-1-4303-2446-1
Library of Congress:	

07

Ennovation Press, Inc.
PO Box 46462
Madison, WI 53717-6462
U.S.A.

To arrange bulk purchase discounts for sales promotions, premiums, or fund-raisers, please contact Lulu Press, Corp or SSIC Publishing, Corp. at the above address. For Information on translation or book distributors outside the U.S.A., please contact us at the above address.

Understanding SQL Server 2008

Copyright © 2008 by Ennovation Press, Inc (Publisher); All rights reserved, Printed in the United States of America. Except as permitted under the Copyright Act of 1976, no part of this publication may be reproduced or distributed in any form or by any means, or stored in a database or retrieval system, without the prior written permission of the Publisher.

Second Edition
978-1-4303-2446-1

Information has been obtained by Publisher from sources believed to be reliable. However, because of the possibility of human or mechanical errors by our sources, Publisher, or others, Publishers does not guarantee to the accuracy, or completeness of any information included in this work and is not responsible for any errors or omissions or the results obtained from the use of such information

Ennovation Press, Inc.; does not make any representations or warranties as to the accuracy, adequacy, or completeness of any information contained in this Work, and is not responsible for any errors or omissions.

About this Book

The idea behind this book is simple. I want you the reader/student to be able to see technology solutions, not technology systems. At times we get so focus on the mechanics of an idea that we tend to forget or ignore the big picture; what I call the business driven force or spirit of any technology based enterprise solution.

Therefore, my strategy for this book is to provide you with the technological foundation needed to understand emerging technologies. This will take us to the Main Subject of this books with is SQL Server 2005, Framework 2.0-3.0 and the soon to be released Server Core Technology or Windows Longhorn Server.

We will also be discussing other topics, next generation computing and the roles of a Developer, Engineer and Manager who plans to deploy Enterprise or Infra-Structure solutions in the Next 24 to 48 Months. We will first begin with an important Subject, Managing Innovation and Creativity.

Why do we begin our book with this topic? For the reason that businesses are constantly looking for innovative ideas that will put them one step ahead of their competitors it has become important to look far into the future in order to stay "Ahead of the Curve". In other words in order to arrive at a truly new idea, a manager must understand how to manage the innovation process. This book will offer effective managerial strategies that address the organizational aspects of managing a creative team, supporting that creativity, moving an idea to implementation, and troubleshooting ideas to help guide a team through the innovation process.

Managing innovation will not only make you a more valuable manager but will also help successfully navigate your team to implementing the new innovation. One clarification, most of us associate innovation with new product development or deployment. However, I challenge you to think of your new SQL Server or Server Framework deployment as part of an innovation process.

A manager needs to understand the creative process and effectively allow for creativity to happen if he wants his team to create something that will set the company apart from the competition

SQL Server Supporting Technology

How to Use This Book

Each chapter covers one broad topic or set of related topics. Each chapter is mean to give you a foundation on the technology your interested on deploying, in this manner I help you create a strong foundation in which you can based deployment decision on. The chapters are arranged in order of increasing proficiency; skills you acquire in one chapter are used and developed in subsequent chapters. For this reason, you should work through the chapters in sequence, although the information on each chapter could be used stand alone also.

I have organized each chapter into results-oriented topics. Topics include all the relevant and supporting information you need to master *SQL Server 2005 and Visual Studio.Net 2005 including MIIS 2007, Framework 2.0-3.0 and Server Core (Longhorn) technology. Activities or Labs found in this book, will allow* you to apply this information to practical hands-on examples.

At times I will use several business scenarios. These business scenarios immerse you in a comfortable environment where you are presented with situations that require you to make real world decisions based on the principles you have learned in the course of this book.

Within these simulations, you will meet characters, have access to clear and timely feedback, and have the ability to review and change previous decisions. These business simulations are available on the course CD-ROM and can be accessed from any computer having the software and hardware requirements specified in the Course Requirements section of your manual.

As a Review Tool

Any method of instruction is only as effective as the time and effort you are willing to investing it. In addition, some of the information that you learn in class may not be important to you immediately, but it may become important later on. For this reason, we encourage you to spend some time reviewing the topics and activities after the course. For an additional challenge when reviewing activities, try the "Why To Do It" column before looking at the "How To Do It" column.

As a Reference

The organization and layout of the book make it easy to use as a learning tool and as an after class reference. You can use this book as a first source for definitions of terms, background information on given topics, and summaries of procedures.

SQL Server Supporting Technology

Table of Contents

About this Book 5
How to Use This Book 6
As a Review Tool 6
As a Reference 6
Introduction 16
HTML 16
What is HTML? 16
Elements in HTML Documents 17
Empty Elements 17
Upper and Lower Case 17
Elements Attributes 17
XML is just like HTML? 18
W3C Recommendation 18
HTML vs. XML 19
XML 20
Why use XML? 20
XML Goals? 22
   The XML specification sets out the following goals for: 22
XML Technologies 24
Choosing XML 24
Introduction 28
XML Tag 28
Element 28
Empty Element Syntax 28
Root Element 28
Child Element 29
Parent Element 29
XML - Tree Structure 29
XML Tree Rules 30
Ancestor 31
Determining Ancestry 31
Descendant 32
   lemonade.xml: 33
Sibling 33
Finding Your Siblings 34
   lem.xml: 34
Element Review 34

SQL Server Supporting Technology

WELL-FORMED	34
XML PARSER	35
WHITESPACE	35
XML DECLARATION	35
GENERATED XML	36
CREATING XML ELEMENTS	36
ADDING ATTRIBUTES	36
ATTRIBUTE	37
ATTRIBUTE USAGE	37
ATTRIBUTE VS. ELEMENT	37
CREATING AN ATTRIBUTE	38
INSERTING XML ENTITIES	38
XML ENTITIES	38
ENTITY	39
ENTITY DECLARATION	39
CREATING AN XML ENTITY	40
INSERTING ENTITIES	40
XML DOCUMENTS	40
PROCESSING INSTRUCTION	41
PROCESSING INSTRUCTION SYNTAX	41
COMMENT	41
GUIDELINES (CDATA) TAG	42
IMPLEMENT NAMESPACES	42
WHAT IS A URI?	43
NAMESPACE	43
DECLARATION SYNTAX	43
GUIDELINES FOR NAMESPACES	44
INTRODUCTION	48
VALIDATE XML WITH A DTD	48
WHAT IS A DTD?	48
DOCTYPE DECLARATION	48
XML Validation	*49*
Valid or Well-Formed	*50*
• *Well-Formed XML*	*50*
• *One Root Element*	*50*
• *Proper Nesting*	*50*
• *Well-Formed Entities*	*50*
Broken XML	*50*
Well-Formed XML	*50*
Valid XML	*51*

SQL Server Supporting Technology

Broken XML Files *51*
ASSIGNING AN EXTERNAL DTD 51
CREATING A DTD 52
   Element Type Declaration *52*
   Attribute List Declaration *52*
   General Entities *53*
ENTITY LIST DECLARATION 53
INTERNAL GENERAL ENTITY 53
   Internal Entity Declaration *53*
   Syntax *53*
   DTD *54*
   XML *54*
   Parameter Entities *54*
CREATING A DTD 54
   Validate XML with a Schema *55*
XML SCHEMA 55
   Limitations of a DTD *55*
   Schema of Schema's *56*
VALIDATING SCHEMA'S 56
   Schema Assignment Syntax *57*
VALIDATING XML WITH A SCHEMA 57
CREATING A SCHEMA 57
   The <schema> *57*
   The <element> *57*
   Common Datatypes *58*
INTRODUCTION 60
   Web applications *60*
   Data exchange *60*
   Application integration *60*
XML DOCUMENT STRUCTURE 60
XML DECLARATION 60
   Defining Elements *61*
   Defining Elements *61*
   Abbreviated Syntax Elements *61*
   Defining Attributes *62*
DEFINING TEXT CONTENT? 62
UNDERSTANDING NAMESPACES 62
   Xml Namespaces *64*
   Namespace Declarations *64*
DEFINING A NAMESPACE 66

SQL Server Supporting Technology

DEFAULT NAMESPACE	67
NON-DEFAULT NAMESPACE	67
NAMESPACES FUTURE	68
SUMMARY	69
INTRODUCTION	72
WHAT IS AN OBJECT?	72
Class	73
Object	73
What are properties?	74
What is a Method?	74
Message passing	74
Inheritance	74
Encapsulation	75
Abstraction	76
Polymorphism	76
What is API?	77
What is the DOM?	77
What is a Node Objects?	77
ACCESS XML BY USING THE (DOM)	78
SIMPLE API FOR XML (SAX)	78
SAX	78
SAX parsing	79
Common SAX Objects	79
Manipulating XML with (SAX)	81
XML ELEMENT OVERLAP	84
XML NAMESPACE SYNTAX	85
NAMESPACE QUALIFICATION	86
Wrong Namespace	86
Correct Namespace	86
DEFAULT NAMESPACE	88
DEFAULT NAMESPACE AND ATTRIBUTES	89
UN-DECLARING NAMESPACE	89
NO NAMESPACE	90
SUMMARY	91
WHAT IS XSL-T?	94
XSLT - KNOW YOUR XPATH!	95
XSLT EXAMPLE	95
XML CODE:	95
XSLT CODE:	95
XSLT SYNTAX	97

SQL Server Supporting Technology

- *XSLT Declaration* 97
- *XSLT Code (Work in Progress!):* 97
- *XSLT Code* 97
- *XSL: Namespace Prefix* 98
- *Syntax Overview* 98
- **STYLESHEET REFERENCE** 98
- **XML-STYLESHEET** 98
  - *xsl:template* 99
  - *xsl:template Match Attribute* 99
- **WHAT IS XQUERY?** 102
  - *What You Should Already Know* 102
  - *What is XQuery?* 102
  - *XQuery and XML* 103
  - *XQuery Defined* 104
  - *An Expression Language* 105
  - *XQuery Conditional Expressions* 106
  - *The result:* 106
  - *Self Evaluation* 107
  - *XQuery Comparisons* 107
  - *Node Values and Expressions* 108
  - *Creates* 109
  - *Sequences* 109
  - *Iterating Over Sequences* 111
- **XQUERY USER-DEFINED FUNCTIONS** 113
  - *Syntax* 113
- **GUIDE FOR USER-DEFINED FUNCTIONS:** 113
- **SORTING AND CONTEXT** 114
- **TYPE SPECIFICATION** 114
- **ADD HTML ELEMENTS AND TEXT** 115
- **ADD ATTRIBUTES TO HTML ELEMENTS** 116
- **SELECTING AND FILTERING ELEMENTS** 117
- **THE FOR CLAUSE** 117
  - *Result:* 117
  - *Result:* 118
  - *Result:* 118
- **THE LET CLAUSE** 118
  - *Result:* 118
- **THE WHERE CLAUSE** 119
- **THE ORDER BY CLAUSE** 119
  - *Result:* 119

SQL Server Supporting Technology

THE RETURN CLAUSE	119
Result:	119
FLWOR EXPRESSIONS	119
GENERAL GUIDELINES:	120
THINGS NOT COVERED HERE:	121
XML DATABASES	121
Native XML processing is:	121
Relational XML processing is:	121
XML SHREDDING	121
Collection	122
Recipe	122
Ingredient	122
Preparation	122
Step	123
Comment	123
Nutrition	123
FROM XQUERY TO SQL	123
MIXED PROCESSING	124
Shredding with fine XML fragments:	124
Shredding with coarse XML fragments:	124
WHAT IS XPATH?	126
WHAT YOU SHOULD ALREADY KNOW	126
XPATH - FINDING INFORMATION	126
XPATH - USED IN XSLT	127
WHAT IS XPATH?	127
XPATH PATH EXPRESSIONS	127
XPATH STANDARD FUNCTIONS	127
XPATH IS USED IN XSLT	127
XPATH - ELEMENT	128
XPATH TERMINOLOGY	128
ATOMIC VALUES	129
ITEMS	129
RELATIONSHIP OF NODES	129
CHILDREN	129
SIBLINGS	129
ANCESTORS	130
DESCENDANTS	130
XML EXAMPLE	131
RELATIVE LOCATION	131
XPATH EXPRESSION:	131

SQL Server Supporting Technology

SELECTING NODES	131
Examples	*132*
PREDICATES	133
Examples	*133*
SELECTING UNKNOWN NODES	134
Examples	*134*
SELECTING SEVERAL PATHS	134
Examples	*134*
XML EXAMPLE	135
XPATH AXES	135
LOCATION PATH EXPRESSION	136
A SIMPLE XPATH EXPRESSION	137
XPATH OPERATORS	138
THE XML EXAMPLE DOCUMENT	139
SELECTING NODES	140
SELECT ALL BOOK NODES	140
Select the First book Node	*140*
A Workaround!	*140*
Select the prices	*140*
XPath Summary	*141*
What's Next?	*141*
*Vertical Bar	(Pipe)*	*141*
Combining Two Expressions with |	*141*
Combining XPath Expression:	*142*
Combining XPath Expression:	*142*
XML IN A SQL SERVER 05-08	145
APPLICATIONS	146
TRADITIONAL XML HANDLING	147
PARAMETERS WITH XQUERY	151
EXECUTING THE XQUERY	155
Summary	*157*
INTRODUCTION	160
PROTECT INFORMATION SECURITY	160
INFORMATION SECURITY	160
HACKERS AND CRACKERS	160
USER ID AND PASSWORD	161
ACCESS RIGHTS	161
PROTECT INFORMATION SECURITY	161
BACKING-UP DATA	162
IMPLICATIONS OF THEFT	162

SQL Server Supporting Technology

PREVENTING A VIRUS ATTACK 163
COMPUTER VIRUSES 163
ANTIVIRUS SOFTWARE 164
LIMITATIONS OF ANTIVIRUS 164
PREVENTING A VIRUS ATTACK 165
   Threat and Vulnerability Mitigation (Database Engine 2008) 165
INTRODUCTION 168
   Security and Data Auditing 168
   Availability and Reliability 168
   Performance 168
MANAGEMENT 169
NEW DATA TYPES 169
DEVELOPMENT ENHANCEMENTS 170
SERVICE BROKER 170
CONVERSATION PRIORITY 171
DATA WAREHOUSING/ETL 171
REPORTING 172
DEPRECATION 172
LOG LOGICAL ARCHITECTURE 174
LOGICAL OPERATION LOGGED 174
LOG PHYSICAL ARCHITECTURE 175
   Write-Ahead Transaction Log 177
   Query Processor Architecture 186
   Linked Servers 186
   Common Language Runtime (CLR) 187
   DBCC 187
   Dynamic Management Views 188
   Transact-SQL 188
INTRODUCTION 191
FEATURES NOT SUPPORTED IN THE NEXT VERSION OF SQL SERVER 191
   Features Not Supported in a Future Version of SQL Server 194

CHAPTER 1

Introduction to XML

In this chapter, you will examine the process of moving from idea to implementation.

You will:

- Determine when to use XML
- Refine ideas.
- Decide to implement or abandon an idea.
- Troubleshoot during the implementation phase.

Introduction

You have used HTML to develop Web pages. Since HTML is a presentation only language it has its limitations. Now you would like to deploy your content to more than just the Web. In this chapter, you will explore the capabilities of XML. Recognizing the capabilities of various markup languages can help you identify the best tool for your project.

Understanding when to use XML rather than another markup language is the first step in creating your development project.

HTML

The **HyperText Markup Language (HTML)** is a markup language that is the Web standard for online publishing. It consists of a limited set of predefined tags used to contain and format content that is displayed in a Web browser. HTML can be developed using simple text editors. It can be viewed in any browser and, because most Web browsers are free, HTML is very easy to deploy. However, even though HTML is platform independent, it can be extended to include proprietary tags from software companies that will display only in their specific Web browsers.

What is HTML?

HTML is designed to specify the logical organizational presentation layer language, this tag base language allows the developer to display content in a webpage, and however it has browser based limitation. This choice was made because the same HTML document may be viewed by many different "browsers", of very different abilities. For example one browser may indent the beginning of a paragraph, whereas a different browser may only leave a blank line.

HTML divides the text of a document into blocks called *elements*. These can be divided into two broad categories -- those that define how the BODY of the document is to be displayed by the browser, and those that define information `about' the document, such as the title or relationships to other documents.

- HTML stands for **H**yper **T**ext **M**arkup **L**anguage
- An HTML file is a text file containing small **markup tags**
- The markup tags tell the Web browser **how to display** the page
- An HTML file must have an **htm** or **html** file extension

- An HTML file can be created using a **simple text editor**

Elements in HTML Documents

The HTML instructions, along with the text to which the instructions apply, are called HTML *elements*. The HTML instructions are themselves called *tags*, and look like <element_name> -- that is, they are simply the element name surrounded by left and right angle brackets.

Most elements mark blocks of the document for particular purpose or formatting: the above <element_name> tag marks the beginning of such as section. The end of this section is then marked by the *ending* tag </element_name> -- note the leading slash character "/" that appears in front of the element name in an end tag. End, or stop tags are always indicated by this leading slash character.

For example, the heading at the top of this page is an H2 element, (a level 2 heading) which is written as:

<H2> 2.1 Elements in HTML </H2>.

Empty Elements

Some elements are *empty* -- that is, they do not affect a block of the document in some way. These elements do not require an ending *tag*. An example is the <HR> element, which draws a horizontal line across the page. This element would simply be entered as

<HR>

Upper and Lower Case

Element names are case *insensitive*. Thus, the horizontal rule element can be written as any of <hr>, <Hr> or <HR>.

Elements Attributes

Many elements can have arguments that pass parameters to the interpreter handling this element. These arguments are called *attributes* of the element. For example, consider the element A, which marks a region of text as the beginning (or end) of a hypertext link. This element can have several attributes. One of them, HREF, specifies the hypertext document to which the marked piece of text is linked. To specify this in the tag for A you write:

<A HREF= "http://www.somewhere.ca/file.html"> marked text </a>.

where the attribute HREF is assigned the indicated value. Note that the A element is not empty, and that it is closed by the tag </a>. Note also that end tags *never* take attributes -- the attributes to an element are always placed in the start tag.

XML is just like HTML?

The answer to this question is simple NO, Why? They are related since they have the same foundation or grandparent's nothing more than derived from the same ancestors. In order for you to understand the relationship between XML and HTML let first look at what HTML is.

HTML is the acronym which defines HTML (*Hyper Text Markup Language RFC 1866*), which started as a small application of **SGML** for the Web, originating with Tim Berners-Lee at CERN in 1989–90. It defines a very simple class of report-style documents tags, with section headings, paragraphs, lists, tables, and illustrations, with a few informational elements, but very few presentational elements, plus some hypertext and multimedia.

W3C Recommendation

The World Wide Web consortium (W3C) specifies rules to a technology that has been approved by the W3C committee members. A technology achieving status as a *W3C recommendation* probably already is or will become the Web standard for its specific function

The W3C, (World Wide Web Consortium) in conjunction with browser vendors and the **WWW** community, began to set policies to avoid browser collisions.

The browser wars of the 90's is a great example of how inflexible HTML can be, since both Microsoft and Netscape unique variance on the HTML tags created a very unstable environment for web application deployment.

Today in 2007 most browsers understand XML and use an XML Set to create platform independency when needed. HTML has now become the presentation layer of the application concentration on how data is displayed not how it is queried.

This is of paramount importance for end users who want to deploy solutions in the World Wide Web, since compatibility conflicts will continue until the two browser manufacturers call it a truth, therefore an incompatibility exist between Netscape and Internet Explorer.

HTML vs. XML

Although both HTML and XML use tags to provide markup for data on the Web, they have a number of important differences.

As a markup language, HTML provides a fixed set of tags that you can use to provide formatting information to Web browsers. Alternatively, XML is a meta-markup language with no tags of its own, so you can use it to create new markup languages that describe data in a meaningful way.

HTML documents contain tags that provide the browser with information about how the data should be displayed. The set of tags allowed in an HTML document is well defined and fixed. You cannot define new types of elements in HTML.

```
<TABLE>
    <TR>
       <TD>Name</TD> Elsa </TD>
    </TR>
    <TR>
       <TD>Salary</TD>78000</TD>
    </TR>
    <TR>
       <TD>Region</TD><TD>Louisiana</TD>
    </TR>
</TABLE>
```

For example, the following HTML displays data in a two-column table. However, it does not dictate the type of data in the table.

XML describes how data is structured, not how it should be displayed or used. XML documents contain tags that assign meaning to the content of the document. These tags allow parsing applications to find the data they need within the XML document.

For example, the following XML contains information about an employee but does not dictate how to display the data:

```
<employee>

    <name>Elsa</name>
    <salary>78000</salary>
    <region>Louisiana</region>
```

```
</employee>
```

XML

The **Extensible Markup Language (XML)** is a markup language that has self-describing tags, has structural guidelines, and can be displayed online. It can be used to create other markup languages. XML is *extensible*, or has the ability to evolve by modifying or adding features. XML, through its associated technologies, can be molded to display in multiple mediums, such as print and online. XML can be displayed across nonproprietary systems and applications. The content and format of the data are separate, allowing an XML document to be formatted in many different ways.

Why use XML?

In order to appreciate XML, it is important to understand why it was created. XML was created so that richly structured documents could be used over the web. The only viable alternatives, HTML and SGML, are not practical for this purpose.

XML is a derived language. Oddly enough XML and HTML both share the same parent SGML. Therefore, XML expresses all the flexibility of HTML while being able to breach the platform issues, how? By becoming a type of wrapper for HTML tags.

Since XML specifies neither semantics nor a tag set. Matter of fact as we said previously XML is really a meta-language for describing markup languages the flexibility is limitless.

In other words, XML provides a facility to define tags and the structural relationships between them. Since there's no predefined tag set, there will never be any preconceived semantics.

Therefore, XML becomes a platform independent bridge to alleviate the issues with cross-browser implementations of Web Technology. All of the semantics of an XML document will either be defined by the applications that process them or by stylesheets.

Here are a few reasons for using XML (in no particular order). Not all of these will apply to your own requirements, and you may have additional reasons not mentioned here (if so, please let the editor of the FAQ know!).

SQL Server Supporting Technology

- XML can be used to describe and identify information accurately and unambiguously, in a way that computers can be programmed to 'understand' (well, at least manipulate as if they could understand).

- XML allows documents which are all the same type to be created consistently and without structural errors, because it provides a standardized way of describing, controlling, or allowing/disallowing particular types of document structure. [Note that this has absolutely nothing whatever to do with formatting, appearance, or the actual text content of your documents, only the structure of them.]

- XML provides a robust and durable format for information storage and transmission. Robust because it is based on a proven standard, and can thus be tested and verified; durable because it uses plain-text file formats which will outlast proprietary binary ones.

- XML provides a common syntax for messaging systems for the exchange of information between applications. Previously, each messaging system had its own format and all were different, which made inter-system messaging unnecessarily messy, complex, and expensive. If everyone uses the same syntax it makes writing these systems much faster and more reliable.

- XML is free. Not just free of charge (free as in beer) but free of legal encumbrances (free as in speech). It doesn't belong to anyone, so it can't be hijacked or pirated. And you don't have to pay a fee to use it (you can of course choose to use commercial software to deal with it, for lots of good reasons, but you don't pay for XML itself).

- XML information can be manipulated programmatically (under machine control), so XML documents can be pieced together from disparate sources, or taken apart and re-used in different ways. They can be converted into almost any other format with no loss of information.

- XML lets you separate form from content. Your XML file contains your document information (text, data) and identifies its structure: your formatting and other processing needs are identified separately in a stylesheet or processing system.

The two are combined at output time to apply the required formatting to the text or data identified by its structure (location, position, rank, order, or whatever).

One final note I must point out before moving on. XML is not a programming language; I stated this in a prior sentence. XML only purpose is to give structure to raw data, much like RDBMS gives structure to databases.

In later chapters we will talk about XSL and XSLT which are use to transform raw xml. XSLT is the programming side of XML.

XML Goals?

The XML specification sets out the following goals for:

- It shall be straightforward to use XML over the Internet.

  - Users must be able to view XML documents as quickly and easily as HTML documents. In practice, this will only be possible when XML browsers are as robust and widely available as HTML browsers, but the principle remains.

- XML shall support a wide variety of applications.

  - XML should be beneficial to a wide variety of diverse applications: authoring, browsing, content analysis, etc. Although the initial focus is on serving structured documents over the web, it is not meant to narrowly define XML.

- XML shall be compatible with SGML.

  - Most of the people involved in the XML effort come from organizations that have a large, in some cases staggering, amount of material in SGML. XML was designed pragmatically, to be compatible with existing standards such as SGML, while solving the relatively new problem of sending richly structured documents over the web.

- It shall be easy to write programs that process XML documents.

  - The colloquial way of expressing this goal is that it ought to take about two weeks for a competent computer science graduate student to build a program that can process XML documents.

- The number of optional features in XML is to be kept to an absolute minimum, ideally zero.

  - Optional features inevitably raise compatibility problems when users want to share documents and sometimes lead to confusion and frustration.

- XML documents should be human-legible and reasonably clear.

  - If you don't have an XML browser and you've received a hunk of XML from somewhere, you ought to be able to look at it in your favorite text editor and actually figure out what the content means.

- The XML design should be prepared quickly.

  - Standards efforts are notoriously slow. XML is needed to solve problems that exist *right now* so time is of the essence.

- The design of XML shall be formal and concise.

  - In many ways a corollary to rule 4, it essentially means that XML must be expressed in EBNF and must be amenable to modern compiler tools and techniques.
  - There are a number of technical reasons why the SGML grammar *cannot* be expressed in EBNF. Writing a proper SGML parser requires handling a variety of rarely used and difficult to parse language features. XML does not.

- XML documents shall be easy to create.

  - Although there will eventually be sophisticated editors to create and edit XML content, they won't appear immediately. In the interim, it must be possible to create XML documents in other ways: directly in a text editor, with simple shell and Perl scripts, etc.

- Terseness in XML markup is of minimal importance.

  - Several SGML language features were designed to minimize the amount of typing required to manually key in SGML documents. These features are not supported in XML.

From an abstract point of view, these documents are indistinguishable from their more fully specified forms, but supporting these features adds a considerable burden to the SGML parser (or the person writing it,

anyway). In addition, most modern editors offer better facilities to define shortcuts when entering text.

XML Technologies

XML has various associated technologies that add to its extensibility and use.

Choosing XML

A well-chosen markup language takes into consideration all project specifications and objectives and weighs them against the strengths and weaknesses of each of the tools available. The most appropriate markup language for implementing any project will accommodate project presentation requirements and meet project objectives.

Characteristics for determining when to use a specific markup language are as follows:

- Choose XML for your project if:

SQL Server Supporting Technology

- The project specifications require distribution and presentation in multiple environments.

- The expertise and software available or required are XML-oriented.

- You need to create self-describing tags to contain your content more clearly.

- Implementation needs to be across non-proprietary systems and browsers.

• Choose HTML for your project if:

- The project needs to be displayed only on the Internet using **Web pages**.

- The expertise and software available or required are **HTML-oriented**.

- The project is small and needs to be displayed online quickly.

- The format of the project is a higher priority than the content *itself*.

- The expertise and software available or required are SGML-oriented.

- Requirements do not include the integration of the Web or its technologies.

- Documents requiring links between them are not included.

SQL Server Supporting Technology

CHAPTER 2

Introduction to XML

In this chapter, you will create a well-formed XML document

You will:

- Create XML elements within a new XML document.
- Create an XML element attribute.
- Insert XML entities to display syntax characters within an XML document.
- Create additional XML components within a well-formed XML document that add to the extensibility and clarity.
- Implement namespaces to eliminate ambiguity in an XML document.

Introduction

You have reviewed the requirements for the output and have determined that XML is the markup language to use. Now you need to start developing. In this chapter, you'll learn how to create a working XML document.

A well-formed document is the foundation of an XML project. Without a document being well-formed, you can't even display your content.

XML Tag

A tag is just a generic name for a <element>. An opening tag looks like <element>, while a closing tag has a slash that is placed before the element's name: </element>. From now on we will refer to the opening or closing of an element as open or close tags. All information that belongs to an element must be contained between the opening and closing tags of an element.

Element

An **element** is a markup component that contains data. An XML element consists of a start and end tag that indicate the element name. Any data between the start and end tag is also considered part of the element. An XML element can have any name without special characters, spaces, or beginning with the letters "xml." This name must be exactly the same in both the start and end tag. An element can contain other elements, content only, or it can be empty.

    <ElementName>   </ElementName>

Empty Element Syntax

An empty element uses only a single tag with a closing mark. A closing tag is not necessary. Empty elements are used specifically for those elements that contain no data, yet have an attribute.

    <ElementName *attributeName="value"*/>

Root Element

A **root** element is an element that contains all other elements and data within an XML document. Sometimes referred to as the document element, there can be only one root element in an XML document.

Child Element

Elements that are opened and closed within another element are said to be child elements.

```
<elementName>
    <childElement>
    </childElement>
</elementName>
```

Parent Element

Elements that have child elements, or children, are defined as parent elements. The root element is parent to all other elements in an XML document.

```
<rootElement>
    <parentElement>
        <childElement>
        </childElement>
    </parentElement>
</rootElement>
```

You may have seen a lot of XML material make references to descendants, children, parents or even great grandchildren and wondered to yourself, "Am I reading a family tree or am I learning XML?" The terminology that XML uses to describe the various relationships in a document can be confusing at first, which is why we wrote a set of chapters to clearly explain and show the most commonly used relation terms.

XML - Tree Structure

The great benefit about XML is that the document itself describes the structure of data. If any of you have researched your family history, you have probably come across a family tree. At the top of the tree is some early ancestor and at the bottom of the tree are the latest children.

With a tree structure you can see which children belong to which parents, which grandchildren belong to which grandparents and many other relationships.

SQL Server Supporting Technology

The neat thing about XML is that it also fits nicely into this tree structure, often referred to as an XML Tree.

Before you even think about matching up these tree terms with their XML counterparts, it might be helpful to see a real XML document converted into a tree structure. The bookstore.xml document we will be using was created by a particularly enterprising kid to keep inventory of her lemonade stand.

```
<inventory>
    <drink>
        <lemonade>
            <price>$2.50</price>
            <amount>20</amount>
        </lemonade>
        <pop>
            <price>$1.50</price>
            <amount>10</amount>
        </pop>
    </drink>

    <snack>
        <chips>
            <price>$4.50</price>
            <amount>60</amount>
        </chips>
    </snack>
</inventory>
```

As you can see from the XML document, *inventory* is the root element. When we convert the document over to a tree format, we can see that the *inventory* element is at the top of the tree. In other words, all other elements are a descendent of the *inventory* element.

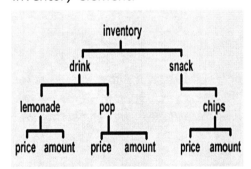

Construction of an XML tree isn't all that hard to do, as long as you follow some basic rules.

XML Tree Rules

We've written up a set of helpful rules to help figure out if an element is a child or parent of another element. With these basic rules you can figure out the relationship of just about any two elements in an XML document.

- **Descendants:** If element A is contained by element B then A is a descendant of B. In the lemonade.xml example every element is a descendant of inventory because inventory is the root element.

- **Ancestors:** If an element B contains element A then B is an ancestor of A. In the lemonade.xml example drink is the ancestor of lemonade and pop.

The next few chapters will go into more detail about: descendant, ancestor, child, parent and sibling relationships in an XML document. If you are still attempting to grasp the notion of the XML Tree structure, we recommend that you carefully read through each of these chapters.

Ancestor

Anyone that came before you, in your family tree, is your ancestor. This means your mom, dad, grandfather, great-great-great-grandmother are all your ancestors.

Although it may seem strange to some, XML has adopted this terminology to define relationships between various XML elements in the same "family". **Element A is the ancestor** of element B if the following is true:

Element B is contained within element A.

Determining Ancestry

If you are trying to eyeball if one element is an ancestor of another element, then you are going to need to find the opening and closing tags of both elements to determine the relationship.

We have highlighted *pop* and *amount* in our lemonade.xml document, **you** must determine which element is the ancestor.

```
<inventory>
    <drink>
        <lemonade>
            <price>$2.50</price>
            <amount>20</amount>
        </lemonade>
        <pop>
            <price>$1.50</price>
            <amount>10</amount>
```

SQL Server Supporting Technology

```
                </pop>
        </drink>

        <snack>
                <chips>
                        <price>$4.50</price>
                        <amount>60</amount>
                </chips>
        </snack>
</inventory>
```

If you said that *pop* was the ancestor of *amount* because *pop* contains *amount* then you're right! Here's a graphical representation of the relationship. If you think of it just like a family tree it becomes a lot easier!

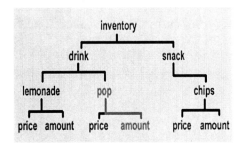

What are the other elements that are the ancestor of the highlighted *amount*? If you said *drink* and *inventory*, that's right! That's because *drink* contains *amount* and *inventory* also contains *amount*.

Tip: The root element of an XML document is the ancestor of every element in the document. This is because all the elements are contained by the root element, by definition of a well-form XML document.

Descendant

Any children that you have are your descendants. Any children that your children have are also your descendants. It doesn't matter how far down the family tree these children are, they will always be your descendants.

A descendant relationship is similar in XML. Element A is the descendant of element B if the following is true:

Element A is contained within element B.

If you are determining if one element is the descendant of another element, then you are going to need to find the opening and closing tags of both elements to determine the relationship.

We have highlighted *inventory* and *lemonade* in our lemonade.xml document, **you must determine which element is the descendant.**

lemonade.xml:

```
<inventory>
    <drink>
        <lemonade>
            <price>$2.50</price>
            <amount>20</amount>
        </lemonade>
        <pop>
            <price>$1.50</price>
            <amount>10</amount>
        </pop>
    </drink>

    <snack>
        <chips>
            <price>$4.50</price>
            <amount>60</amount>
        </chips>
    </snack>
</inventory>
```

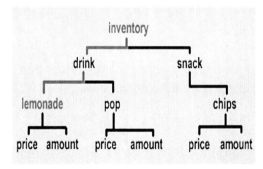

lemonade is the descendant of *inventory*. This situation was a little tricky because lemonade is contained within another element, *drink*. However, it doesn't matter how far down the XML Tree an element is, if it's contained by another element, then it is its descendant.

Here is a graphical representation of the relationship between *inventory* and *lemonade*. You can clearly see that *lemonade* is the descendant.

Sibling

A sibling relationship exists when two elements that have the same parent. There are no brothers or sisters in XML, just simply siblings.

Finding Your Siblings

To find siblings in an XML document look for elements that are on the same level of the tree **and** have the same parent.

Who is the sibling of *snack*?

lem.xml:

```
<inventory>
    <drink>
        <lemonade>
            <price>$2.50</price>
            <amount>20</amount>
        </lemonade>
        <pop>
            <price>$1.50</price>
            <amount>10</amount>
        </pop>
    </drink>

    <snack>
        <chips>
            <price>$4.50</price>
            <amount>60</amount>
        </chips>
    </snack>
</inventory>
```

drink is the sibling of *snack*.

If you look at the tree structure you can clearly see that the elements *drink* and *snack*, of the lemonade.xml document, share the same parent, *inventory*.

Element Review

Elements are used to classify data in an XML document so that the data becomes "self-explanatory". Opening and closing tags represent the start and end of an element. Attributes are used to include additional information on top of the data that falls between the opening and closing tag.

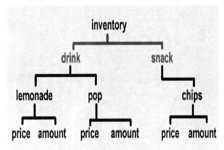

Well-formed

Well-formed is a structural requirement of all XML documents that allows XML to be consistently formed across systems and browsers. For an XML document to be well-formed, it must meet the following rules:

- The document must contain at least one element.

- The document must contain one element that contains all other elements, the root element.

- All elements in the XML document must have matching start and end tags that are case-sensitive. The only exception is that of an empty element.

All elements must be nested properly within one another.

XML Parser

To modify or read an XML document, you need an XML parser. An XML parser checks the well-formed of an XML document and sometimes more. There are many XML parsers available, but the parser that XMLSPY uses by default in its Home edition is the MSXML parser. This parser supports the specification of XSLT and XPath technologies, as well as improvements on the accommodations for SAX and DOM. By using the check for well-formed command in XMLSPY, you are activating the parser.

Whitespace

Adding whitespace to the markup doesn't affect the document's content, but adding whitespace to the data between tags does. Typically, whitespace will be added to indent child elements. This makes your XML easier to read.

XML Declaration

An XML declaration is an XML component found at the beginning of an XML document that defines the document to be an XML markup that conforms to the W3C specification. An XML declaration is not necessary for well-formed, but it is good practice to always include it at the beginning of every XML document. The XML declaration contains a version attribute with a value of 1.0, which is the current and only version of XML. The declaration can also include an encoding attribute whose common value is UTF-8. It begins and ends with question marks within the beginning and closing angle brackets. The XML declaration is not an element.

SQL Server Supporting Technology

Generated XML

Visual Studio.Net 2005 support XML development when creating an XML document the Studio will automatically generates the XML declaration <?xml version="1.0" encoding="UTF-8"?> for you. When creating an XML document in a text editor, you would have to type the declaration. Another way of creating the XML code is to write it in Notepad, however is you do it there you must remember to place the XML directives at the top of the page.

Creating XML Elements

1. To create an element in an XML document:

2. Open or create the XML document that you wish to insert an element into.

3. If you are using an XML editor, consult the editor-specific directions on how to open a new XML document type. If you are using a text editor, remember to save your document with an .xml extension.

4. Place the insertion point in the location where you will insert your element.

5. Type a proper start tag to begin your element.

6. Type a proper end tag to end your element.

7. As necessary, insert any data and child elements that may be contained within the element.

8. Check for well-formed.

9. Test the document in a Web browser.

10. If necessary, format the document so that it is easier to view the nested element structure.

11. Save the document

Adding Attributes

You have created elements to contain the content of your XML document. Another method of collecting and containing this information is using an attribute. In this topic, you will create XML attributes.

Some of the data stored in your XML document may not be critical to the structure, yet still be necessary to include in the content. Although a separate element can contain this information, an attribute may be more appropriate.

Attribute

An attribute is a markup component that contains data further describing element data. An attribute is part of an XML Element and it is found in the Element tag declaration.

Attribute usage

Attributes are used to specify additional information about the element. It may help to think of attributes as a means of specializing generic elements to fit your needs. An attribute for an element appears within the opening tag.

If there are multiple values an attribute may have, then the value of the attribute must be specified. For example, if a tag had a color attribute then the value would be: red, blue, green, etc. The syntax for including an attribute in an element is:

    <element attributeName="value">

In this example we will be using a made-up XML element named "friend" that has an optional attribute age.

Attribute vs. Element

The correct storage component for data within an XML document depends heavily on both the intent of the XML document and your role as a developer. Even though both components can effectively contain any content, choosing the appropriate container for your content will allow you to structure your data efficiently so that you can easily understand and locate information within your XML document. Characteristics for determining where to store XML content are as follows: Store your content in an element if:

- The content is crucial to the structure of the document.
- The content is critical to the role or purpose of the project.

Store your content in an attribute if:

- The content is an aspect or characteristic of an element.
- The content is a name or number used to reference an element.
- You want to give a certain limited number of values to choose from.

Creating an Attribute

To create an attribute for an XML element:

1. If necessary, create an element for your attribute to describe.
2. Place the insertion point inside the element start tag and immediately before the closing bracket. Insert a space.
3. Type the attribute name.
4. Insert an equal sign (=).
5. Insert the value of the attribute within quotation marks. If the attribute is empty, put nothing in between the quotations.
6. Check for well-formed.
7. Test by viewing in a Web browser.
8. Save your XML document.

Inserting XML Entities

You have created components to contain and describe data within an XML document. Although creating elements and attributes are the most common tasks you will perform, they aren't the only components that add functionality to your document. In this topic, you will create

XML entities

In order to display special characters such as the angle brackets, the ampersand, and quotation marks that are also used in markups, you will need to insert built-in entities into your XML document.

Entity

An *entity* is a string of characters that represents a reserved XML character or repetitive text. Entities allow you to use XML markup characters, such as the less-than symbol (<), as content in your XML document and are inserted into an XML document instead of the information they represent when an XML document is parsed. If you use an XML markup character as text in your code, the file will not be well-formed.

Entity Declaration

This syntax uses an entity in an XML document:

    <elementName>&entity;</elementName>

The ampersand indicates that the text following it is an entity. The semicolon signifies the end of the entity.

With symbolic representation of information, a lot of text, such as, "Hello my name is Tizag.com and I am an artificial intelligence that teaches the general public how to program in web languages for free" can be represented by an entity symbol.

You may have used entities in the past. The format of an entity in XML is an ampersand(&), followed by the name of the symbol, and concluded with a semicolon.

Generic Entity - &name;

HTML is another markup language that supports entities. Below are some example entities and the information they represent.

© = ©
< = <
> = >
® = ®

Creating an XML Entity

An entity must be created in the Document Type Definition (DTD). When you know where to place the entity, the rest is easy. Here is the syntax for creating your own XML entities.

<!ENTITY entityName "The text you want to appear when the entity is used">

Below we have created an entity for the default introduction we want to include on all of our documents.

Inserting Entities

Procedure Reference: Insert a Built-in Entity

To insert a built-in entity within an XML document:

1. If necessary, create the element in which the built-in entity is to be inserted.

2. Place the insertion point inside the appropriate element, between the start and end tags.

3. Insert any data and the appropriate built-in entity that will output the character you desire.

4. Check for well-formed.

5. Test the XML document in a browser to verify that the built-in entity character is displayed.

6. Save the document.

XML Documents

You have been creating various components of the XML structure. Although you have created elements, attributes, and entities, there are other components that may or may not appear within the context of an XML document. In this topic, you will create additional XML document components.

The simplest XML documents contain only elements and attributes. But, suppose you need to enter a bulk amount of data with several characters of markup into the content of your document. To do this or other special tasks, you will use XML tools designed for the job.

Processing Instruction

A processing instruction is an XML component that allows you to include separate files or instructions that are to be processed by the application that uses the XML file. They are not used by the XML parser. The parser passes the processing instruction to the application, and how the separate information is interpreted is up to the application.

Processing Instruction Syntax

This syntax creates a processing instruction that an application uses to apply an stylesheet to an XML document:

```
<?xml-stylesheet type="text/type" href="path to stylesheet"?>
```

To create a processing instruction to process a CSS document, the type attribute's value is "text/css".

Comment

You have used comments in HTML and they serve the same purpose in XML: to explain what the code does so others who use your code can better understand it. Comments are not necessary for the creation and validation of an XML document and are ignored by the XML parser. Comments are created with the same syntax as in HTML:

XML comments have the exact same syntax as HTML comments. Below is an example of a notation comment that should be used when you need to leave a note to yourself or to someone who may be viewing your XML.

```
<?xml version="1.0" ?>
```

```
<!-- Students grades are updated bi-monthly -->
<class_list>
    <student>
        <name>Roberto</name>
        <grade>C</grade>
    </student>
    <student>
        <name>Jose</name>
        <grade>B-</grade>
    </student>
</class_list>
```

Guidelines (CDATA) Tag

To create a CDATA section in your XML document:

If necessary, create the element in which the CDATA section will be included.

1. Place the insertion point where you wish to insert the character data.
2. Insert <![CDATA[to declare that character data will follow. Type the information and insert]]> to end the character data tag.
3. If necessary, format your document to word wrap.
4. Check for well-formed.
5. Verify your document in a browser.
6. Verify your document in a browser.
7. 7. Save the document.

Implement Namespaces

You have created various components in a single XML document. However, there are special concerns when working with multiple documents with the same element name. In this topic, you will implement namespaces.

At times, you may need to integrate distinct XML documents into one large source document.

During this process, you may notice elements having the exact same name, yet containing very different information. By implementing XML namespaces, you can eliminate any potential confusion, creating the single source document with both elements.

SQL Server Supporting Technology

What is a URI?

A **Universal Resource Identifier (URI)** is a short string that uniquely identifies a resource, typically on the Web. It can point to a specific resource, such as a file, or other types of objects. URIs are most commonly Uniform Resource Locators (URLs).

Namespace

A *namespace* is a classification technique that uniquely identifies elements and attributes. Namespaces prevent elements and attributes that have the same name as other elements and attributes from conflicting with each other. A namespace must be declared using the xmlns attribute before elements can be assigned to it. A prefix (can be any characters other than XML markup) is assigned to each namespace when multiple namespaces are used in a document. Namespaces are usually declared within the document's root element. The namespace is identified by a URI.

The XML namespace is a special type of *reserved XML attribute* that you place in an XML tag. The reserved attribute is actually more like a prefix that you attach to any namespace you create. This *attribute prefix* is "**xmlns:**", which stands for XML NameSpace. The colon is used to separate the prefix from your namespace that you are creating.

As we mentioned in our XML Attribute Chapter, every XML attribute **must** be set equal to something. *xmlns* must have a unique value that not other namespace in the document has. What is most commonly used is the URI (Uniform Resource Identifier) or the more commonly used URL.

To rectify the overlap in our *health* XML document we will be using the W3C's XHTML URL and a made up URI for our second *body* element. Both the namespace attribute and its use in our document has been highlighted in red.

Declaration Syntax

    <elementName xmlns:*prefix="URI">*

An element is assigned to a namespace by creating the element with the appropriate prefix that matches a namespace's prefix. Such elements are called Qualified or Namespace Qualified names.

```
<?xml version="1.0"
<html:html xmlns:html='http://www.w3.org/TR/xhtml1/'>
<html:body>
<html:p>Welcome to my Health Resource</html:p>
</html:body>
<H:body xmlns:health='http://www.example.org/health'>
      <H:height>6ft</height>
      <H:weight>155 lbs</weight>
</H:body>
</html:html>
```

Guidelines for Namespaces

To implement namespaces in an XML document:

- If necessary, insert any appropriate content.

- If necessary, insert the start tag for the root element. If you are creating a new XML document, you will need to insert the start tag for the root element.

- Place the insertion point immediately after the name of the root element and immediately before the ending angle bracket. Insert a space to separate the name and namespace declaration.

- Insert xmlns: to state that the following code is an XML namespace.

- Create a short prefix referencing your first URI (it should probably be 1–3

- characters).

- Insert =.

- In quotation marks, insert the URI that you are referencing.

- Insert any remaining namespaces that will be used in the document using the xmlns: declaration and another unique prefix.

- If necessary, close the tag. You will need to close the tag if you have just created a new root element.

- For each element in the document referenced using namespacing, insert the prefix followed by a colon immediately before the name of the element in the start tag.

SQL Server Supporting Technology

- Check for well-formed XML
- Save the document.

SQL Server Supporting Technology

CHAPTER 3

Validating an XML Document

In this chapter, you will validate an XML document.

You will:

- Validate an XML document with a Document Type Definition.
- Create a DTD so that XML documents are validated.
- Validate XML with a schema.

Create a schema based on the current W3C recommendation.

Introduction

You have created well-formed XML documents based on project specifications. Until your XML documents have been verified, they will not be useable. In this chapter, you will validate an XML document.

Validating a document verifies that all content, and their types, are appropriately structured and present. Assuring that a document is valid maintains consistency with all XML documents of that type.

Validate XML with a DTD

Your well-formed XML document has been created and is ready to be validated. The simplest method of validation is using a Document Type Definition (DTD). In this chapter, you will validate XML with a Document Type Definition (DTD).

Since XML is used to create your own markup language, you will need rules that enable the markup language to be understood semantically. The DTD serves as the document's rules of grammar. Without validating a document against a DTD, the markup language you develop could simply be speaking in gibberish.

What is a DTD?

A Document Type Definition (DTD) is a set of rules that verifies the structure of markup in XML document types. DTDs are the simplest and most original method of verifying XML documents. An external DTD is located separately from the XML, and is used to validate one or more documents. An internal DTD is embedded inside an XML document and validates only the XML document it is located in. DTDs describe the existence, occurrence, and structure of elements, attributes, and entities within a specific XML document type.

DOCTYPE Declaration

A DOCTYPE declaration is a DTD component stating that the XML document is validated by a DTD. A DOCTYPE declaration either includes an internal DTD, or gives the location of an external DTD file. A DOCTYPE declaration should be located immediately following the XML declaration, before the root element.

SQL Server Supporting Technology

XML Validation

XML validation is when a validating parser checks the structure and content of an XML document type against its assigned DTD or schema.

Number	Stage Name	Description
1	Well-formed verification	The first step in validating an XML document is to check for well-formed. If the document is well-formed, the process continues.
2	Assignment of validation	Document verification In this stage, the validating parser verifies that the XML document type has been assigned to a DTD or some other validation technology; for example, checking for an accurate DOCTYPE declaration.
3	Structural verification	After correct assignment, the validating parser verifies that all structural elements, such as elements and attributes, written in the DTD or other validation document, are present in the XML document. It verifies that the proper order and occurrence in the XML match those described in the DTD. Also, the parser verifies the appropriate data is in the right location.
4	Valid output	If all of the previous stages return no errors, then the document is said to be valid.

Valid or Well-Formed

In XML there are three ways to measure a document's correctness: valid, well-formed, and broken. You probably only care that your XML document works, but knowing the requirements for each kind of correctness may shed some light on problems that arise in the future.

- Well-Formed XML

    A well-formed XML document has to follow several rules that most other markup languages also follow. These are generic rules that must be followed for a document to be well-formed, as well as valid. The rules are as follows:

- One Root Element

    The XML document may only have one root element. See our Root Element chapter for more information.

- Proper Nesting

    XML elements must be closed in the order they are opened. See our Nesting chapter for more information.

- Well-Formed Entities

    Any entities that are referenced in the document must also be well formed. See our Entity chapter for more information.

    The first example below is incorrect and the second is well-formed. Try to figure out the error that is in the first example.

Broken XML

```
<email>
    <to>Mr. Garcia
        <body>Hello there! How are we today?</to>
    </body>
</email>
```

Well-Formed XML

```
<email>
    <to>Mr. Garcia</to>
    <body>Hello there! How are we today?</body>
</email>
```

The error in the first example was:

The document suffers from improper nesting. The body element was opened inside the to element, yet body was not closed before the to element was closed!

Valid XML

First and foremost, a valid XML document must be well-formed before it can even think about being a valid XML document. The well-formed requirement (see above) should be fairly straightforward. The key to making an XML document leap from well-formed to valid is slightly more difficult.

To be valid an XML document must be validated. A document cannot be validated unless a Document Type Definition (DTD), internal or external, is referenced for the XML processor. For the XML document to be valid, it must follow all the rules set forth in the DTD.

Broken XML Files

Broken XML documents are simply those which fail to follow the rules required for a document to be either well-formed or valid. Many of the XML editors on the market today (free and purchased) are an excellent source of help when attempting to fix small errors in your XML code.

Assigning an External DTD

1. If necessary, delete any embedded DTD syntax.

2. Place the insertion point before the root element.

3. Insert the code <!DOCTYPE to begin the document type declaration, then insert a space.

4. Type the name of the root element.

5. Insert the code SYSTEM to declare the location of the DTD.

6. Type the URI location of the DTD for your file in quotations.

7. Close the document type declaration by typing an end angle bracket.

8. Check for well-formed.

9. Check validity.

10. If necessary, make any changes to validate your XML file(s) and check again for validity.

11. Save the document.

Creating a DTD

You have now validated an XML document against its DTD. By creating your own DTD, you are describing the structural guidelines in which your document type would be considered valid. In this topic, you will create a DTD.

By learning the DTD syntax, you can begin to describe the element and attribute structure for your XML document type. Once the DTD is created, other documents of the same type must follow the predefined organization of your DTD. Processes, such as outputting your document, become easier because all valid documents written against your DTD will have a determined composition.

Element Type Declaration

An element type declaration is a DTD component that declares the existence of an element within an XML document type. The declaration can also include operators that describe the sequence of child elements and indicators that define the occurrence for each of these elements.

Attribute List Declaration

An attribute list declaration is a DTD component that declares the existence of an attribute within an XML document type. The declaration includes the type and default value, if necessary, of the attribute.

The **attribute-type** can be one of the following:

Type	Description
CDATA	The value is character data
(en1|en2|..)	The value must be one from an enumerated list
ID	The value is a unique id
IDREF	The value is the id of another element
IDREFS	The value is a list of other ids
NMTOKEN	The value is a valid XML name
NMTOKENS	The value is a list of valid XML names
ENTITY	The value is an entity
ENTITIES	The value is a list of entities

NOTATION	The value is a name of a notation
xml:	The value is a predefined xml value

The **default-value** can be one of the following:

Value	Explanation
Value	The default value of the attribute
#REQUIRED	The attribute is required
#IMPLIED	The attribute is not required
#FIXED *value*	The attribute value is fixed

General Entities

A general entity is an entity that creates a shorthand notation of frequently used text inside an XML document type. An internal general entity is declared in the DTD and states replacement text to be inserted in the XML document type. An external entity is also declared in the DTD but refers to information or a file outside of the DTD. By defining general entities, frequently used text can be referenced without re-typing the original data at every occurrence.

Entity List Declaration

An *entity list declaration* associates a shorthand name for frequently used text in a DTD. You must declare an entity before it can be used in the XML or DTD syntax.

Internal General Entity

To declare an internal entity to be used in the XML document, use the following DTD syntax.

Entities are variables used to define shortcuts to standard text or special characters.

- Entity references are references to entities
- Entities can be declared internal or external

Internal Entity Declaration

Syntax

```
<!ENTITY entity-name "entity-value">
```

<!ENTITY entity-name SYSTEM "URI/URL">

DTD

<!ENTITY Date SYSTEM "http://www.sample.com/entities.dtd">
<!ENTITY Month SYSTEM "http://www.sample.com/entities.dtd">

XML

<Year>&Date;&Month;</Year>

Parameter Entities

A parameter entity is an entity that creates a shorthand notation of frequently used text inside a DTD. It is used to represent DTD content and make the task of writing the DTD easier. A parameter entity can be both internal and external. It must be declared using an entity declaration in the DTD.

Creating a DTD

1. If necessary, create a new DTD file.

2. Starting with the root element, define any element type declarations for all elements in the XML document.

    a. Type <!ELEMENT to begin an element declaration.

    b. Insert the name of the element.

    c. Within parentheses, list and separate all child elements using the appropriate operator.

    d. Identify the occurrence of each child element using the appropriate indicator.

    e. Type an end angle bracket > to end the element type declaration.

3. After all elements have been declared, define any attribute list declarations for all attributes in the XML document.

    f. Type <!ATTLIST to begin an attribute list declaration.

    g. Insert the name of the element that the attribute describes.

    h. Insert the name of the attribute.

    i. Insert the attribute datatype.

    j. Insert the default value of the attribute.

k. Type an end angle bracket > to end the attribute list declaration.

4. After the DTD has been created, check for well-formed.

5. Save the DTD.

6. If necessary, assign the DTD to any XML document types.

7. Validate each XML document against the DTD to be certain that all guidelines have been met and the documents are formed correctly.

8. Save XML document types.

Validate XML with a Schema

You have checked validity of XML documents with a DTD. DTDs are simple to create for a well-formed XML document, yet they lack the extensibility of XML. In this topic, you will validate XML with a schema.

DTDs have limitations. As XML is being used more and more, these limitations are becoming more apparent. While DTDs are more than adequate for describing documents, they come up short when it comes to describing data. The XML schema is a more powerful XML validating technology.

XML Schema

A schema is a set of rules that verifies the structure of markup in XML document types. The XML schema recommendation was adopted on May 2, 2001 by the W3C.

XML schemas are written as well-formed XML documents. They can use namespaces and are extensible. Compared to DTDs, schemas are better able to describe what kind of data is contained in an element or attribute.

Limitations of a DTD

XML schemas were created to overcome the limitations of DTDs and accommodate the needs of developers.

- DTDs are written in a syntax different than XML. Hence, DTDs are not extensible themselves; they simply add to the extensibility of XML.

- DTDs have no support for namespaces.

- DTDs have no support for strong data type. For example; string, integer, and date.

- DTDs do not support inheritance. Therefore, a DTD cannot be a sub-class of another DTD.

Schema of Schema's

Every valid XML document has an assigned DTD or schema. Because XML schemas are composed in XML, the schema dialect itself has a validating schema document to verify its structure. The schema of schemas is located at http://www.w3.org/2001/XMLSchema.

Validating Schema's

An error message will occur and the validation process will stop if a problem occurs. These error messages are dependent on the editor or validating parser you are using.

Problem	Description
Data type mismatch	This occurs when content in the XML document does not match the declared type in the assigned schema.
Missing namespace	When the namespace for the schema location and schema-instance is incorrectly formed, is misspelled, or is missing in the XML root element.
Missing element	When an element declared in an XML document's assigned schema is not present, is misspelled, or is incorrectly formed in the XML.
Missing attribute in XML	When an attribute declared in an XML document's assigned schema is not present, is misspelled, or is incorrectly formed in the XML.
Incorrect element type	When an element is declared as complex in the schema, but occurs differently in the XML

Schema Assignment Syntax

To assign a schema to an XML document, the syntax of the root element must be modified to include the namespace of the schema of schemas and the URI location of the validating schema.

Validating XML with a Schema

1. Place the insertion point inside of the root element start tag, after the name.
2. Declare the namespace instance for W3C schemas.
3. Insert the code to declare the location of the schema.
4. Type the URI location of the schema for your file in quotations.
5. Check for well-formed.
6. Check for validity.

Creating a Schema

You have now validated an XML document against its schema. To validate your personal document type using the most powerful method, you will need to develop a schema. In this topic, you will create a schema.

Developing a schema is the most powerful and extensible option to validate your document type. For example, say you receive a call from your supervisor to design a DTD or schema for a textbook client. When you notice restricted data typing, such as requiring the publication dates to be in specific formats, the pages having to be numbered, and inserting true or false values for revisions of the text, you automatically know that the weak data descriptive powers of DTDs are not the solution.

The <schema>

The <schema> element, or preamble, is an element found in a schema that is the root of every schema. It may provide the schema's name and the type.

The <element>

The <element> element is a schema element that declares the name of an XML element. It can include occurrence attributes used to declare how many times the element can appear in the XML as a child element. The <element> element can also include the type attribute when describing an element that contains data only.

Attribute	Description
maxOccurs	Indicates the maximum number of times the element can occur within its parent element. The value can be an integer 0 or greater, though a value of "unbounded" can be used to indicate no limit. This attribute is not allowed if the parent is the <schema> element.
minOccurs	Indicates the minimum number of times the element can occur within its parent element. The value can be an integer 0 or greater, with 0 indicating that the element is optional. This attribute is not allowed if the parent is the <schema> element.
name	The name of the element; for instance, a value of "book" would declare the XML element <book>.
ref	A reference pointer to an element declared elsewhere in the schema, or another schema whose namespace has been referenced. This attribute is not allowed if the parent is the <schema> element.
type	The datatype of the element.

Common Datatypes

Even though there are many more, a table of the most commonly used datatypes in schemas has been provided. These are the values that would be entered in the typeattribute of an element or attribute declaration.

CHAPTER 4

Representing Data with XML

In this chapter, you will create a well-formed XML document

You will:

- Learn how to represent Data
- Review the overall structure as introduced in the previous chapter

SQL Server Supporting Technology

Introduction

In this section, you will learn how to represent data in an XML document. You will learn about the overall structure of an XML document, and see how to use XML elements, attributes, and text content to hold the document data.

In addition, you will learn how to use XML namespaces to qualify element names and attribute names.

Web applications

You will see how to build sophisticated and efficient Web applications by using XML documents to represent the information flow between a Web server and a Web browser.

Data exchange

You will see how XML documents can promote and simplify business-to-business (B2B) e-commerce, to allow trading partners to exchange documents in a common format.

Application integration

You will see how XML can enable asynchronous messaging between loosely coupled business applications. When transferring data from one business application to the next, XML can be used to encode both the content of the data and the routing information.

XML Document Structure

A well-formed XML document contains the following parts: an XML declaration, a single document element, any number of child elements,

any number of attributes, text content, and zero or more namespace declarations. We will examine each of these parts in detail in this section.

XML Declaration

Each XML document starts with an XML declaration, which indicates the version of the XML document and the character set encoding in the document.

Example:

```
<?xml version="1.0" encoding="UTF-8"?>
```

Defining Elements

An XML document must have a single container element, called the document element. All other elements and text content must be defined between the start and end tags of the document element, as shown in the following example.

```
<employees >
        <employee_ID/>
        <Address> Data </Address>
        <City/>
        <State/>
        <Zip/>
</employees>
```

Defining Elements

Elements are the most important part of an XML document. You define elements in a hierarchy, to reflect the organization of the data you want the XML document to hold. Most elements are coded by using a start and end tag, and contain relevant text data.

In this example, employee data is encoded by using XML. The elements that contain name and pay-rate data use start and end tags.

```
<employee>
        <name>Debbie</name>
        <payrate>32.50</payrate>
</employee>
```

Abbreviated Syntax Elements

Sometimes, you may wish to define an element that has no child elements or text content. This typically happens when the presence of the element itself is enough to convey the meaning of the data.

In this example, the <employee> element has a child element named <contractor> The contractor element has no additional content, so it uses the abbreviated element syntax.

```
<employee>
        <name>Debbie</name>
```

```
            <payrate>32.50</payrate>
            <contractor/>
</employee>
```

Defining Attributes

You can define attributes within the start tag of an element, to provide more information about an element.

In this example, the employee identification number and the start date of employment are encoded by using attributes of the <employee> element.

```
<employee id="123" start="1997">
        <name/>
        <Department/>
        <Salary/>
</employee>
```

Defining Text Content?

You can define text content between the start and end tags of an element.

```
<employee>

        <id>123</id>
        <start>1997</start>

        <name>Nataniel Simon</name>
        <department>Accounting</department>
        <salary>$59,000</salary>

</employee>
```

Understanding Namespaces

XML namespaces provide a method for uniqueness, which differentiates between multiple schema authors who use the same element names. Namespaces qualify the names of XML elements and XML attributes in XML document instances. A qualified name consists of a prefix and a local name, separated by a colon.

The prefix functions only as a placeholder; it is mapped to a Uniform Resource Identifier (URI) that specifies a namespace. The combination of the universally managed URI namespace and the local name produces a name that should be universally unique.

Let me begin by saying that namespaces have been a W3C standard since January 1999. The though behind namespaces is simple: We need a way to fully qualify XML element and attribute names to prevent from confusing two elements that have the same name but mean different things.

However I must make an annotation. XML Namespaces and .Net Namespaces although similar in concept are different in implementation. A Visual Studio.Net Namespace it is not the something as an XML Namespace as specified by the W3C. Having said this let look at why we use namespaces in the first place.

As we said above namespaces identify the meaning and origin of XML data. Another example to consider is the following a company has an accounting application that uses an element called <schedule> to mean an accounting schedule.

However a time management application potentially could also use the same element called <schedule> to mean a time schedule. As the accountant you might need to put accounting and time management data in one XML document. Potentially this will create a problem since in XML all tags as we learn in previous chapters must be unique in order to be well-form XML.

For example, you might be keeping track of all project information including accounting and project timeline in the same document. Now each application would not be able to tell which <schedule> element belongs to it.

To solve this problem, you could prefix each <schedule> element with a unique prefix that indicates to which application it belongs. For example <accounting:schedule> and <time:schedule> would make things much clearer. In this example accounting and time are namespaces.

One of the primary motivations for defining an XML namespace is to avoid naming conflicts when using and re-using multiple vocabularies.

XML Schema is used to create a vocabulary for an XML instance, and uses namespaces heavily. Thus, having a sound grasp of the namespace concept is essential for understanding XML Schema and instance validation overall.

Xml Namespaces

As XML usage on the Internet became more widespread, the benefits of being able to create markup vocabularies that could be combined and reused similarly to how software modules are combined and reused became increasingly important. If a well defined markup vocabulary for describing coin collections, program configuration files, or fast food restaurant menus already existed, then reusing it made more sense than designing one from scratch.

Combining multiple existing vocabularies to create new vocabularies whose whole was greater than the sum of its parts also became a feature that users of XML began to require.

However, the likelihood of identical markup, specifically XML elements and attributes, from different vocabularies with different semantics ending up in the same document became a problem. The very extensibility of XML and the fact that its usage had already become widespread across the Internet precluded simply specifying reserved elements or attribute names as the solution to this problem.

The goal of the W3C XML namespaces recommendation was to create a mechanism in which elements and attributes within an XML document that were from different markup vocabularies could be unambiguously identified and combined without processing problems ensuing.

The XML namespaces recommendation provided a method for partitioning various items within an XML document based on processing requirements without placing undue restrictions on how these items should be named. For instance, elements named <template>, <output>, and <stylesheet> can occur in an XSLT stylesheet without there being ambiguity as to whether they are transformation directives or potential output of the transformation.

An XML namespace is a collection of names, identified by a Uniform Resource Identifier (URI) reference, which are used in XML documents as element and attribute names.

Namespace Declarations

A namespace declaration is typically used to map a namespace URI to a specific prefix. The scope of the prefix-namespace mapping is that of the element that the namespace declaration occurs on as well as all its children. An attribute declaration that begins with the prefix xmlns: is a namespace declaration.

Here is an example of an XML document where the root element contains a namespace declaration that maps the prefix bk to the namespace name urn:xmlns:25hoursaday-com:bookstore and its child element contains an inventory element that contains a namespace declaration that maps the prefix inv to the namespace name urn:xmlns:25hoursaday-com:inventory-tracking.

```
<bk:bookstore xmlns:bk="urn:xmlns:25hoursaday-com:bookstore">
  <bk:book>
    <bk:title>Lord of the Rings</bk:title>
    <bk:author>J.R.R. Tolkien</bk:author>
    <inv:inventory status="in-stock" isbn="0345340426"
        xmlns:inv="urn:xmlns:25hoursaday-com:inventory-tracking" />
  </bk:book>
</bk:bookstore>
```

In the above example, the scope of the namespace declaration for the urn:xmlns:25hoursaday-com:bookstore namespace name is the entire bk:bookstore element, while that of the urn:xmlns:25hoursaday-com:inventory-tracking is the inv:inventory element. Namespace aware processors can process items from both namespaces independently of each other, which leads to the ability to do multi-layered processing of XML documents.

It should be noted that by definition the prefix xml is bound to the XML namespace name and this special namespace is automatically pre-declared with document scope in every well-formed XML document.

Thus, we see that the namespaces in XML concept is not very different from packages in Java. This correlation is intended to simplify the understanding of namespaces in XML and to help you visualize the namespaces concept.
In this Chapter you will learn:

- The role of namespaces in XML

- How to declare and use namespaces

- The difference between default-namespace and no-namespace

- How to create namespaces using XML Schema,

- The difference between qualified and unqualified elements/attributes in a namespace.

Namespaces are simply a way to uniquely identify elements and attributes within a document.

Namespaces are similar to packages in Java in several ways:

- A package can have many reusable classes and interfaces. Similarly, a namespace in XML can have many reusable elements and attributes.

- To use a class or interface in a package, you must fully qualify that class or interface with the package name. Similarly, to use an element or attribute in a namespace, you must fully qualify that element or attribute with the namespace.

- A Java package may have an inner class that is not directly inside the package, but rather "belongs" to it by the virtue of its enclosing class.

The same is true for namespaces: there could be elements or attributes that are not directly in a namespace, but belongs to the namespace by virtue of its parent or enclosing element. This is a transitive relationship. If a book is on the table, and the table is on the floor, then transitively, the book is on the floor; albeit the book is not *directly* on the floor.

Therefore, as you can see the namespaces in XML concept is not very different from packages in Java. This correlation is intended to simplify the understanding of namespaces in XML and to help you visualize the namespaces concept

A Microsoft namespaces behaves in the same manner it uses a Unique Resource Identifiers (URIs) to identify the meaning of elements and attributes in an XML document. A URI can be any globally unique string.

Defining a Namespace

Understanding XML namespaces is essential to understanding and building Web services. Unfortunately, most developers do not understand how XML namespaces work and get confused when they see all the colons and URLs. The funny thing is, namespaces are so simple that once you understand them you wonder why you had trouble understanding them in the first place.

Namespaces identify the meaning and origin of XML data. Organizations often use similar names to represent common business information. For example, two companies might create an XML grammar with an element named <employee>. However, the internal structure of the <employee> element might be very different in each case. A solution is implementing a namespace and therefore the XML tags will be unique for example:

<ssic.employee> or <microsoft.employee>

Each company that produces XML documents can include a reference to the namespace on a document, to indicate the origin and meaning of the XML data. Namespaces are described in detail in the following section. There are two ways to define a namespace in an XML document:

- Define a default namespace.

- Define a non-default namespace.

Default Namespace

Default namespaces are useful when you want all or most of an XML document to have the same namespace.

A default namespace is defined as follows.

<element-name **xmlns=**"*namespace-URI*"*>*

This namespace definition applies to the current element and all of its descendants. Typically, default namespace declarations are placed in themdocument element. In this case, the namespace applies to all of the content in the entire document.

This example declares a default namespace in the document element. The namespace applies to all elements and attributes in the document.

```
<?xml version="1.0"?>
<employees xmlns="urn:SoftwareSolutionsCorp">
...document-content...
</employees>
```

Non-Default Namespace

Non-default namespaces are useful when you want some parts of a document to be in a namespace, and other parts in a different namespace. A non-default namespace is defined as follows.

<prefix:element-name xmlns:prefix="namespace-URI">

A non-default namespace applies to elements or attributes that are qualified with the namespace prefix. Unqualified elements and attributes are not part of the namespace.

This example declares a non-default namespace in the document element. The namespace prefix is **hr**, and the namespace URI is:

"urn:SoftwareSolutionsCorp".

The <employee> and <name> elements are qualified with the namespace prefix and therefore are part of the namespace. The <B> element is not qualified, so it is not part of the namespace.

```
<?xml version="1.0"?>

<hr:employees xmlns:hr="urn: SoftwareSolutionsCorp ">
<nw:employee>
<nw:name> Rigoberto <B>Garcia</B> </hr:name>
</nw:employee>
</nw:employees>
```

Namespaces Future

There are a number of developments in the XML world focused on tackling some of the issues that have developed around XML namespaces. Firstly, the current draft of the W3C XML namespaces recommendation does not provide a mechanism for undeclaring namespaces that have been mapped to a prefix. The W3C XML namespaces v1.1 working draft is intended to rectify this oversight by providing a mechanism for undeclaring prefix namespace mappings in an instance document.

The debate on what should be returned on an attempt to dereference the contents of a namespace URI has lead to contentious debate in the XML world and is currently the focus of deliberations by the W3C's Technical Architecture Group. The current version of the XML namespaces recommendation does not require the namespace URI to actually be resolvable because a namespace URI is supposed to merely be a namespace name that is used as a unique identifier, and not the location of a resource on the Internet.

Tim Bray (one of the original editors of both the XML Language and XML namespaces recommendations) has written an exhaustive treatise on the issues around namespace URIs and the namespace documents that may or may not be retrieved from them. This document contains much of the reasoning that was behind his creation of the Resource Directory Description Language (RDDL), which is designed to be used for creating namespace documents.

SUMMARY

- The scope of a declared namespace begins at the element where it is declared and applies to all the elements within the content of that element, unless overridden by another namespace declaration with the same prefix name.

- Both prefixed and {default namespace} can be overridden.

- Both prefixed and {default namespace} can be undeclared.

SQL Server Supporting Technology

CHAPTER 5

Accessing XML Documents with APIs

In this chapter, you will access XML documents with APIs. You will:

- Access an XML document using DOM.
- Manipulate XML data using SAX.

SQL Server Supporting Technology

Introduction

You have created and validated XML documents in order to store and display data. Once you have a valid XML document, you can modify and retrieve specific data stored in that document. In this chapter, you will access an XML document to modify and retrieve data.

Suppose a user wants to find a particular piece of information in a long XML document. The user could open the XML file and begin scrolling the file line by line until the information is located. However, this is very inconvenient and time-consuming. Accessing XML documents using APIs enables users to programmatically find the specific data more efficiently.

Once an XML document is created, an automated approach involving an API is often used to access the file. The Document Object Model (DOM) is one of the most commonly used APIs because of the number of ways it can be used. In this topic, you will access an XML document using DOM.

Most companies have document information that needs to be updated. For example, new health care rates take effect on the first of each year at most companies. A member of the company's human resources department needs to reflect the new rates in the employee benefits documentation. By using an application designed to work with DOM, the human resources department can make changes to the information in the XML document by adding, deleting, or updating data.

What is an Object?

An *object* is a software entity that has characteristics and performs actions. **Object-oriented programming** (OOP) is a programming paradigm that uses "objects" and their interactions to design applications and computer programs. It is based on several techniques, including encapsulation, modularity, polymorphism, and inheritance.

It was not commonly used in mainstream software application development until the early 1990s. Many modern programming languages now support OOP.

Object oriented programming roots reach all the way back to the 1960s. As hardware and software became increasingly complex, researchers studied how software quality could be maintained. Object-oriented programming was deployed in part as an attempt to address this problem by strongly emphasizing discrete units of programming logic and re-usability in software.

SQL Server Supporting Technology

The Simula programming language was the first to introduce the concepts underlying object-oriented programming (objects, classes, subclasses, virtual methods, coroutines, garbage collection, and discrete event simulation) as a superset of Algol. Simula was used for physical modeling, such as models to study and improve the movement of ships and their content through cargo ports. Smalltalk was the first programming language to be called "object-oriented".

Object-oriented programming may be seen as a collection of cooperating *objects*, as opposed to a traditional view in which a program may be seen as a group of tasks to compute ("subroutines"). In OOP, each object is capable of receiving messages, processing data, and sending messages to other objects.

Each object can be viewed as an independent little machine with a distinct role or responsibility. The actions or "operators" on the objects are closely associated with the object. For example, in OOP, the data structures tend to carry their own operators around with them (or at least "inherit" them from a similar object or "class"). The traditional approach tends to view and consider data and behavior separately.

Class

Defines the abstract characteristics of a thing (object), including the thing's characteristics (its **attributes**, **fields** or **properties**) and the thing's behaviors (the **things it can do**, or **methods, operations** or **features**). One might say that a class is a *blueprint* or *factory* that describes the nature of something. For example, the class Dog would consist of traits shared by all dogs, such as breed and fur color (characteristics), and the ability to bark and sit (behaviors). Classes provide modularity and structure in an object-oriented computer program. A class should typically be recognizable to a non-programmer familiar with the problem domain, meaning that the characteristics of the class should make sense in context. Also, the code for a class should be relatively self-contained (generally using **encapsulation**). Collectively, the properties and methods defined by a class are called **members**.

Object

A particular instance of a class. The class of Dog defines all possible dogs by listing the characteristics and behaviors they can have; the object Lassie is one particular dog, with particular versions of the characteristics.

A Dog has fur; Lassie has brown-and-white fur. In programmer jargon, the Lassie object is an **instance** of the Dog class. The set of values of the attributes of a particular object is called its state. The object consists of state and the behavior that's defined in the object's class.

What are properties?

Properties are object component that defines the object's characteristics. Properties store data and/or set values that are part of a particular object. Properties help to distinguish one object from another.

What is a Method?

Metho**ds** are object component that enables objects to perform actions. The type of object determines the actions that are available to it. For example, a dog can bark but a car cannot.

An object's abilities. Lassie, being a Dog, has the ability to bark. So bark() is one of Lassie's methods. She may have other methods as well, for example sit() or eat() or walk(). Within the program, using a method usually affects only one particular object; all Dogs can bark, but you need only one particular dog to do the barking.

Message passing

"The process by which an object sends data to another object or asks the other object to invoke a method." Also known to some programming languages as interfacing; E.g. the object called Breeder may tell the Lassie object to sit by passing a 'sit' message which invokes Lassie's 'sit' method. The syntax varies between languages, for example: [Lassie sit] in Objective-C. In Java code-level message passing corresponds to "method calling".

Inheritance

'Subclasses' are more specialized versions of a class, which *inherit* attributes and behaviors from their parent classes, and can introduce their own.

For example, the class Dog might have sub-classes called Collie, Chihuahua, and GoldenRetriever. In this case, Lassie would be an instance of the Collie subclass. Suppose the Dog class defines a method called bark() and a property called furColor. Each of its sub-classes (Collie, Chihuahua, and GoldenRetriever) will inherit these members, meaning that the programmer only needs to write the code for them once.

Each subclass can alter its inherited traits. For example, the Collie class might specify that the default furColor for a collie is brown-and-white. The Chihuahua subclass might specify that the bark() method produces a high pitch by default. Subclasses can also add new members. The Chihuahua subclass could add a method called tremble().

So an individual chihuahua instance would use a high-pitched bark() from the Chihuahua subclass, which in turn inherited the usual bark() from Dog. The chihuahua object would also have the tremble() method, but Lassie would not, because she is a Collie, not a Chihuahua. In fact, inheritance is an 'is-a' relationship: Lassie *is a* Collie. A Collie *is a* Dog. Thus, Lassie inherits the methods of both Collies and Dogs.

Multiple inheritance is inheritance from more than one ancestor class, neither of these ancestors being an ancestor of the other. For example, independent classes could define Dogs and Cats, and a Chimera object could be created from these two which inherits all the (multiple) behavior of cats and dogs. This is not always supported, as it can be hard both to implement and to use well.

Encapsulation

Encapsulation conceals the functional details of a class from objects that send messages to it. For example, the Dog class has a bark() method. The code for the bark() method defines exactly how a bark happens (e.g., by inhale() and then exhale(), at a particular pitch and volume). Timmy, Lassie's friend, however, does not need to know exactly how she barks. Encapsulation is achieved by specifying which classes may use the members of an object.

The result is that each object exposes to any class a certain *interface* — those members accessible to that class. The reason for encapsulation is to prevent clients of an interface from depending on those parts of the implementation that are likely to change in future, thereby allowing those changes to be made more easily, that is, without changes to clients. For example, an interface can ensure that puppies can only be added to an object of the class Dog by code in that class. Members are often specified as **public**, **protected** or **private**, determining whether they are available to all classes, sub-classes or only the defining class. Some languages go further: Java uses the **default** access modifier to restrict access also to classes in the same package, C# and VB.NET reserve some members to classes in the same assembly using keywords **internal** (C#) or **Friend** (VB.NET), and Eiffel and C++ allows one to specify which classes may access any member.

Abstraction

Abstraction is simplifying complex reality by modelling classes appropriate to the problem, and working at the most appropriate level of inheritance for a given aspect of the problem.

For example, Lassie the Dog may be treated as a Dog much of the time, a Collie when necessary to access Collie-specific attributes or behaviors, and as an Animal (perhaps the parent class of Dog) when counting Timmy's pets.

Abstraction is also achieved through **Composition**. For example, a class Car would be made up of an Engine, Gearbox, Steering objects, and many more components. To build the Car class, one does not need to know how the different components work internally, but only how to interface with them, i.e., send messages to them, receive messages from them, and perhaps make the different objects composing the class interact with each other.

Polymorphism

Polymorphism allows you to treat derived class members just like their parent class' members. More precisely, Polymorphism in object-oriented programming is the ability of objects belonging to different data types to respond to method calls of methods of the same name, each one according to an appropriate type-specific behavior. One method, or an operator such as +, -, or *, can be abstractly applied in many different situations. If a Dog is commanded to speak(), this may elicit a bark(). However, if a Pig is commanded to speak(), this may elicit an oink(). They both inherit speak() from Animal, but their derived class methods override the methods of the parent class; this is Overriding Polymorphism. Overloading Polymorphism is the use of one method signature, or one operator such as '+', to perform several different functions depending on the implementation. The '+' operator, for example, may be used to perform integer addition, float addition, list concatenation, or string concatenation.

Any two subclasses of Number, such as Integer and Double, are expected to add together properly in an OOP language. The language must therefore overload the concatenation operator, '+', to work this way. This helps improve code readability. How this is implemented varies from language to language, but most OOP languages support at least some level of overloading polymorphism. Many OOP languages also support Parametric Polymorphism, where code is written without mention of any specific type and thus can be used transparently with any number of new types.

Pointers are an example of a simple polymorphic routine that can be used with many different types of objects.

Not all of the above concepts are to be found in all object-oriented programming languages, and so object-oriented programming that uses classes is called sometimes class-based programming. In particular, prototype-based programming does not typically use *classes*. As a result, a significantly different yet analogous terminology is used to define the concepts of *object* and *instance*, although there are no *object*s in these languages.

What is API?

An application programming interface is a set of objects that enables an application to communicate with resources such as an operating system, a file, or another application.

It consists of properties and methods that an application uses to create, navigate, or update a resource. One of the benefits of using an API is that application developers can write a program that interacts with the API using their language of choice

What is the DOM?

DOM is an application programming interface that reads an entire XML document into memory and then builds a tree hierarchy of nodes. Each node represents each element in the XML document. The DOM consists of a Node interface, which defines basic properties and methods. DOM allows you to update documents. You can't always use DOM because a document may be too large to efficiently read into memory.

What is a Node Objects?

The DOM contains other types of objects that have their own properties and methods in addition to the properties and methods inherited from the Node interface:

- Attribute
- CDATASection
- Comment\
- Document

- Element
- Entity
- NodeList
- Text

Access XML by using the (DOM)

To access an XML document using DOM:

- Create an application to manipulate the DOM using your language of choice.
- Create an instance of the XML DOM.

Simple API for XML (SAX)

In the previous topic, you accessed an XML document using the DOM API. Depending on the reasons for accessing a document, alternative APIs such as SAX may provide advantages that DOM does not. In this topic, you will manipulate XML data using SAX.

In some cases, manipulating XML documents using SAX instead of DOM results in greater application performance. If an XML document is accessed just to retrieve information, not to modify it, then using SAX is more efficient. If a large XML document needs to be processed, SAX is the way to go, as DOM takes considerably longer to process the document, if it can process it at all.

SAX

SAX is an application programming interface containing properties and methods that developers use to create new XML data. It can also read an existing XML document and translate the content into predefined SAX properties and methods that a developer can work with. SAX is designed to handle large documents but it cannot be used to update them.

SAX parsing

While the parser is reading the XML document it is calling back to user code to tell it what it's encountering. The callbacks occur immediately, before the parser has even determined that the XML document is completely error free.

The advantage of SAX parsing is the user code can ignore what it does not care about and only keep the data it considers important. Thus it can handle huge XML documents. But the disadvantage is the callbacks occur before it's even known if this document is correct XML. If the goal is to analyze the document then the sax user code will often end up writing ad-hoc DOM structure.

Common SAX Objects

SAX contains a number of objects, each with their own properties and methods.

Interface Name	Description
MXXMLWriter	Generates XML output. When connected to SAXXMLReader, accumulates data thrown by the reader.
ContentHandler	Receives the content of a document. Contains methods to create XML content as well.
LexicalHandler	Contains CDATA, comment, DTD, and entity related methods.
SAXXMLReader	Parses an XML document and translates the content into properties and methods.
SAXAttributes	Allows you to create and edit attribute collections.

SAX stands for the Simple API for XML. And simple it really is. Constructing a SAX parser and passing events to handlers is done as simply as:

```
use XML::SAX;
use MySAXHandler;

my $parser = XML::SAX::ParserFactory->parser(
    Handler => MySAXHandler->new  );
```

```
$parser->parse_uri("foo.xml");
```

The important concept to grasp here is that SAX uses a factory class called XML::SAX::ParserFactory to create a new parser instance. The reason for this is so that you can support other underlying parser implementations for different feature sets. This is one thing that XML::Parser has always sorely lacked.

In the code above we see the parse_uri method used, but we could have equally well called parse_file, parse_string, or parse(). Please see XML::SAX::Base for what these methods take as parameters, but don't be fooled into believing parse_file takes a filename. No, it takes a file handle, a glob, or a subclass of IO::Handle. Beware.

SAX works very similarly to XML::Parser's default callback method, except it has one major difference: rather than setting individual callbacks, you create a new class in which to recieve the callbacks. Each callback is called as a method call on an instance of that handler class. An example will best demonstrate this:

```
package MySAXHandler;
use base qw(XML::SAX::Base);

sub start_document {
  my ($self, $doc) = @_;
  # process document start event
}

sub start_element {
  my ($self, $el) = @_;
  # process element start event
}
```

Now, when we instantiate this as above, and parse some XML with this as the handler, the methods start_document and start_element will be called as method calls, so this would be the equivalent of directly calling:

$object->start_element($el);

Notice how this is different to XML::Parser's calling style, which calls:

start_element($e, $name, %attribs);

It's the difference between function calling and method calling which allows you to subclass SAX handlers which contributes to SAX being a powerful solution.

As you can see, unlike XML::Parser, we have to define a new package in which to do our processing (there are hacks you can do to make this uneccessary, but I'll leave figuring those out to the experts). The biggest benefit of this is that you maintain your own state variable ($self in the above example) thus freeing you of the concerns listed above. It is also an improvement in maintainability - you can place the code in a separate file if you wish to, and your callback methods are always called the same thing, rather than having to choose a suitable name for them as you had to with XML::Parser. This is an obvious win.

SAX parsers are also very flexible in how you pass a handler to them. You can use a constructor parameter as we saw above, or we can pass the handler directly in the call to one of the parse methods:

```
$parser->parse(Handler => $handler,
        Source => { SystemId => "foo.xml" });
# or...

$parser->parse_file($fh, Handler => $handler);
```

This flexibility allows for one parser to be used in many different scenarios throughout your script (though one shouldn't feel pressure to use this method, as parser construction is generally not a time consuming process).

Manipulating XML with (SAX)

To read and display XML data using SAX:

1. Create an application using your language of choice.

2. Create an instance of the MXXMLWriter object.

3. Create an instance of the SAXXMLReader object.

4. Set the ContentHandler property of the SAXXMLReader object to the MXXMLWriter object.

    SAXXMLReaderObject*.contentHandler = *MXXMLWriterObject

5. Set the SAXXMLReader object's parseURL method to identify the file to be parsed.

    ***SAXXMLReaderObject*.parseURL(*filePath*)**

6. Use the MXXMLWriter object's output property to display the XML data.

    ***MXXMLWriterObject*.output**

7. Save the application.
8. Test the application.

9. Use the ContentHandler's characters method to assign data to an element.

    ***MXXMLWriterObject*.characters("*characterData*")**

10. Use the ContentHandler's endElement method to close all elements.

    ***objectName*.endElement("*namespaceURI*", "*localName*", "*qualifiedName*")**

11. Implement the ContentHandler's endDocument method to indicate the end of the document.

    ***MXXMLWriterObject*.endDocument()**

12. Use the MXXMLWriter object's output property to display the XML data.

    ***MXXMLWriterObject*.output**

13. If necessary, implement other SAX interface properties and methods to manipulate the XML data.

14. Save the application file.

15. Test the application.

Chapter 6

Recognizing Namespace Conflict

In this chapter, you will develop skills to assess a conflict situation and monitor your reaction to the conflict.

You will:

- Identify your personal reaction to conflict.
- Develop a healthy attitude toward conflict.
- Assess all aspects of the conflict.
- Take measures to avoid conflict escalation.

A namespace is a collection of elements and attribute names identified by a Uniform Resource Identifier reference. The reference may appear in the root element as a value of the "xmlns" attribute.

Namespaces are declared as an attribute of an element. It is not mandatory to declare namespaces only at the root element; rather it could be declared at any element in the XML document.

The scope of a declared namespace at the declaration point, of course this holds true unless the namespace is overridden by another namespace declaration with the same prefix name—where, the content of an element is the content between the <opening-tag> and </closing-tag> of that element. A namespace is declared as follows:

<ElementName xmlns:pfx="http://www.ssic.com" />

The attribute xmlns:pfx, xmlns behaves similar to a reserved word, this unique identifier is used to declare the namespace in order to minimized Element collisions in complex structures. In other words, xmlns is used for bind the Element thru a namespaces, and is not itself bound to any namespace. In the previous code snippet namespace is being bound to the prefix "pfx" with the namespace.

When working with Microsoft technology you will notice a commonly used name space called "XSD". XSD is a convention used XSD to represent the prefix of a Microsoft XML Schema we strongly suggest that this convention is followed in order to create an standardized manner in wich to developed or annotate schemas.

When creating schemas we do have the flexibility to annotate the prefix in any manner we wish, however this annotation should be documented in order to be able to implement RAD (Rapid Application Development) in our development environment

XML Element Overlap

When you are creating new elements, there is the chance that the element's name already exists. Imagine someone was creating a health related XML document that included XHTML (that's HTML that is also valid XML).

```
<?xml version="1.0" encoding="ISO-8859-15"?>
<html>
    <body>
        <p>Welcome to my Health Resource</p>
    </body>

    <body>
```

```
            <height>6ft</height>
            <weight>155 lbs</weight>
      </body>
</html>
```

One question that students often ask me is, why the URL? The answer is simple. The only reason for the URN is to provide syntactical reference for the namespace. Additionally this is used as a container of sorts. This virtual or Ghost "container" is used for documentation or Schema specific vocabulary. These URN becomes a tools to display information or content that can be shared over a network regarles of is location.

Since URN are unique by nature your namespaces should also exhibit this behavior. Namespaces which are not unique can cause problem as the parser begins to validate the XML structure, since namespace collisions might occur.

Here we have two very different elements that want to use the same name: *body*. THe solution to this problem is to create *XML Namespaces*, which will differentiate between these two similarly named elements!

XML Namespace Syntax

The XML namespace is a special type of *reserved XML attribute* that you place in an XML tag. The reserved attribute is actually more like a prefix that you attach to any namespace you create. This *attribute prefix* is "**xmlns:**", which stands for XML NameSpace. The colon is used to separate the prefix from your namespace that you are creating.

As we mentioned in our XML Attribute Chapter, every XML attribute **must** be set equal to something. *xmlns* must have a unique value that not other namespace in the document has. What is most commonly used is the URI (Uniform Resource Identifier) or the more commonly used URL.

To rectify the overlap in our *health* XML document we will be using the W3C's XHTML URL and a made up URI for our second *body* element. Both the namespace attribute and its use in our document has been highlighted in red.

```
      <?xml version="1.0"  ?>
      <html:html xmlns:html='http://www.w3.org/TR/xhtml1/'>
      <html:body>
            <html:p>Welcome to my Health Resource</html:p>
      </html:body>
```

```
<h:body xmlns:health='http://www.example.org/health'>
<h:height>6ft</h:height>
<h:weight>155 lbs</h:weight>
</h:body>
```

```
</html:html>
```

By placing a namespace prefix before our elements we have solved the overlapping problem!

However, one point that must be made understood is that typing the namespace URN(URL) in a browser does not mean it would show automatically all the elements and attributes in that namespace; No, Why? Because as I said before, it is just a syntactical concept; none the less although the W3C Namespaces in XML Recommendation declares that the namespace name should be an IRI, it enforces no such constraint. Therefore, I could also use something like:

```
<MyElement xmlns:pfx="ssic" />
```

Namespace qualification

Some student have asked: why can we not use the namespace to qualify the Elements? Well the answer to this questions is in two parts. The first part is somewhat obvious since the namespaces uses a URN technology for the declaration and URN can be lengthy this would cause tremendous clutter in the code. For this reason it would be impractical to use, since the XML very complex and lengthy.

The second and most important, reason is because it would have a severe negative impact on the syntax, and to be specific, on the production rules of XML. For this reason being that URI could have a myriad of characters which are not allowed in XML version 1.0 as defined by the W3C.

Wrong Namespace

Invalid)
http://www.library.com:Book /

Correct Namespace

Valid)

```
<lib:Book xmlns:lib="http://www.library.com" />
```

Below the elements Title and Author are associated with the Namespace http://www.library.com:

```
<?xml version="1.0"?>
    <Book xmlns:lib="http://www.library.com">
      <lib:Title>Sherlock Holmes</lib:Title>
      <lib:Author>Arthur Conan Doyle</lib:Author>
    </Book>
```

In the example below, the elements Title and Author of Sherlock Holmes – III and Sherlock Holmes - I are associated with the namespace http://www.library.com and the elements Title and Author of Sherlock Holmes - II are associated with the Namespace:

http://www.otherlibrary.com.

```
<?xml version="1.0"?>
<Book xmlns:lib="http://www.library.com">

  <lib:Title>Sherlock Holmes - I</lib:Title>
  <lib:Author>Arthur Conan Doyle</lib:Author>

  <purchase xmlns:lib="http://www.otherlibrary.com">
  <lib:Title>Sherlock Holmes - II</lib:Title>
  <lib:Author>Arthur Conan Doyle</lib:Author>
  </purchase>

  <lib:Title>Sherlock Holmes - III</lib:Title>
  <lib:Author>Arthur Conan Doyle</lib:Author>

</Book>
```

It must be noted that the W3C Namespaces in XML Recommendation and for this reason it enforces some namespace constraints for example:

1. Prefixes beginning with the three-letter sequence x, m, and l, in any case combination, are reserved for use by XML and XML-related specifications.

    a. Although not a fatal error, it is inadvisable to bind such prefixes. The prefix xml is by definition bound to the namespace name http://www.w3.org/XML/1998/namespace.

2. A prefix cannot be used unless it is declared and bound to a namespace.

a. (Ever tried to use a variable in Java without declaring it?)

The following **violates** both these constraints:

```
<?xml version="1.0"?>
<Book xmlns:XmlLibrary="http://www.library.com">
  <lib:Title>Sherlock Holmes - I</lib:Title>
  <lib:Author>Arthur Conan Doyle</lib:Author>
</Book>
```

[Error]: prefix lib not bound to a namespace.
[Inadvisable]: prefix XmlLibrary begins with 'Xml.'

Default Namespace

How cumbersome would it be to repeatedly qualify an element or attribute? Well it would be very impractical. In such cases, you can declare a {default namespace} instead. Remember, at any point in time, there can be only one {default namespace} in existence. Therefore, the term "Default Namespaces" is inherently incorrect.

Declaring a {default namespace} means that any element within the scope of the {default namespace} declaration will be qualified implicitly, if it is not already qualified explicitly using a prefix. As with prefixed namespaces, a {default namespace} can be overridden too. A {default namespace} is declared as follows:

```
<someElement xmlns="http://www.ssic.com" />
```

```
<?xml version="1.0"?>

<Book xmlns="http://www.library.com">
  <Title>Sherlock Holmes</Title>
  <Author>Arthur Conan Doyle</Author>
</Book>
```

In this case the elements Book, Title, and Author are associated with the Namespace http://www.library.com.

Remember, the scope of a namespace begins at the element where it is declared. Therefore, the element Book is also associated with the {default namespace}, as it has no prefix.

```
<?xml version="1.0"?>
```

```xml
<Book xmlns="http://www.library.com">
    <Title>Sherlock Holmes - I</Title>
    <Author>Arthur Conan Doyle</Author>

    <purchase xmlns="http://www.otherlibrary.com">
        <Title>Sherlock Holmes - II</Title>
        <Author>Arthur Conan Doyle</Author>
    </purchase>

    <Title>Sherlock Holmes - III</Title>
    <Author>Arthur Conan Doyle</Author>
</Book>
```

In the above, the elements Book, and Title, and Author of Sherlock Holmes - III and Sherlock Holmes - I are associated with the namespace http://www.library.com and the elements purchase, Title, and Author of Sherlock Holmes - II are associated with the namespace http://www.otherlibrary.com.

Default Namespace and Attributes

Default namespaces do not apply to attributes; therefore, to apply a namespace to an attribute the attribute must be explicitly qualified. Here the attribute isbn has {no namespace} whereas the attribute cover is associated with the namespace http://www.library.com.

```xml
<?xml version="1.0"?>

<Book isbn="1234"
    pfx:cover="hard" xmlns="http://www.library.com"
    xmlns:pfx="http://www.library.com">

 <Title>Sherlock Holmes</Title>
 <Author>Arthur Conan Doyle</Author>
</Book>
```

Un-declaring Namespace

Unbinding an already-bound prefix is not allowed per the W3C Namespaces in XML 1.0 Recommendation, but is allowed per W3C Namespaces in XML 1.1 Recommendation. There was no reason why this should not have been allowed in 1.0, but the mistake has been rectified in 1.1. It is necessary to know this difference because not many XML parsers yet support Namespaces in XML 1.1.

Although there were some differences in unbinding prefixed namespaces, both versions allow you to unbind or remove the already declared {default namespace} by overriding it with another {default namespace} declaration, where the namespace in the overriding declaration is empty.

Unbinding a namespace is as good as the namespace not being declared at all. Here the elements Book, Title, and Author of Sherlock Holmes - III and Sherlock Holmes - I are associated with the namespace http://www.library.com and the elements purchase, Title, and Author of Sherlock Holmes - II have {no namespace}:

```
<someElement xmlns="" />

<?xml version="1.0"?>

<Book xmlns="http://www.library.com">
  <Title>Sherlock Holmes - I</Title>
  <Author>Arthur Conan Doyle</Author>
  <purchase xmlns="">
    <Title>Sherlock Holmes - II</Title>
    <Author>Arthur Conan Doyle</Author>
  </purchase>
  <Title>Sherlock Holmes - III</Title>
  <Author>Arthur Conan Doyle</Author>
</Book>
```

Here's an invalid example of unbinding a prefix per Namespaces in XML 1.0 spec, but a valid example per Namespaces in XML 1.1:

```
<purchase xmlns:lib="">
```

From this point on, the prefix lib cannot be used in the XML document because it is now undeclared as long as you are in the scope of element purchase. Of course, you can definitely re-declare it.

No Namespace

No namespace exists when there is no default namespace in scope. A {default namespace} is one that is declared explicitly using xmlns. When a {default namespace} has not been declared at all using xmlns, it is incorrect to say that the elements are in {default namespace}. In such cases, we say that the elements are in {no namespace}. {no namespace} also applies when an already declared {default namespace} is undeclared.

SQL Server Supporting Technology

SUMMARY

- In order to use a namespace, we first bind it with a prefix and then use that prefix wherever required.

- The scope of a declared namespace begins at the element where it is declared and applies to all the elements within the content of that element, unless overridden by another namespace declaration with the same prefix name.

- Both prefixed and {default namespace} can be overridden.

- Both prefixed and {default namespace} can be undeclared.

- {default namespace} does not apply to attributes directly.

- A {default namespace} exists only when you have declared it explicitly. It is incorrect to use the term {default namespace} when you have not declared it.

- No namespace exists when there is no default namespace in scope.

SQL Server Supporting Technology

CHAPTER 7

Introduction to XSLT

In this chapter, you will secure information.

You will:

- —XSLT Syntax

- —How to apply XSLT with XML for formatting and structure validation

SQL Server Supporting Technology

What is XSL-T?

Now that we are successfully using XML to mark up our information according to our own vocabularies, we are taking control and responsibility for our information, instead of abdicating such control to product vendors. These vendors would rather lock our information into their proprietary schemes to keep us beholden to their solutions and technology.

But the flexibility inherent in the power given to each of us to develop our own vocabularies, and for industry associations, e-commerce consortia, and the W3C to develop their own vocabularies, presents the need to be able to transform information marked up in XML from one vocabulary to another.

Two W3C Recommendations, XSLT (the Extensible Stylesheet Language Transformations) and XPath (the XML Path Language), meet that need. They provide a powerful implementation of a tree-oriented transformation language for transmuting instances of XML using one vocabulary into either simple text, the legacy HTML vocabulary, or XML instances using any other vocabulary imaginable. We use the XSLT language, which itself uses XPath, to specify how an implementation of an XSLT processor is to create our desired output from our given marked-up input.

XSLT enables and empowers interoperability. This XML.com introduction strives to overview essential aspects of understanding the context in which these languages help us meet our transformation requirements, and to introduce substantive concepts and terminology to bolster the information available in the W3C Recommendation documents themselves.

Since April 1999 Crane Softwrights Ltd. has published commercial training material titled Practical Transformation Using XSLT and XPath, covering the entire scope of the W3C XSLT and XPath through working drafts and the final 1.0 recommendations. This material is delivered by Crane in instructor-led sessions and is licensed to other training organizations around the world needing to teach these exciting technologies.

The material presented in this chapter assumes no prior knowledge of XSLT and XPath (*Refer to Chapter in XPath for more detail*s) and guides the reader through background, context, structure, concepts and introductory terminology.

XSLT is an XML-related technology that is used to manipulate and transform XML documents. The acronym XSLT stands for **E**xtensible **S**tylesheet **L**anguage **T**ransformations, which is a mouthful to say, but sounds more complicated than it is.

With XSLT you can take an XML document and chose the elements and values you want, then generate a new file with your choices. Because of XSLT's ability to change the content of an XML document, XSLT is referred to as the *stylesheet* for XML.

If you have already heard about HTML and CSS, you know that CSS is a way of styling HTML. In a similar relationship, XSLT is used to style **and** transform XML.

XSLT - Know Your XPath!

It is virtually impossible to do anything in XSLT without using its sister technology, XPath. Before you can begin XSLT you need to understand the basics of XPath, so if you haven't already, go through our XPath Tutorial.

XSLT Example

To give you an idea of what you'll be learning with XSLT, we've provided a simple XML document that gets transformed by a complicated looking XSLT file.

XML Code:

```xml
<?xml version="1.0" encoding="UTF-8"?>
<?xml-stylesheet type="text/xsl" href="class.xsl"?>

<class>
    <student>Jack</student>
    <student>Harry</student>
    <student>Rebecca</student>
    <teacher>Mr. Bean</teacher>
</class>
```

XSLT Code:

```xml
<?xml version="1.0" ?>
<xsl:stylesheet version="1.0" xmlns:xsl=
    "http://www.w3.org/1999/XSL/Transform">

<xsl:template match="teacher">
<xsl:value-of select="."/>
</xsl:template>

<xsl:template match="student">
<xsl:value-of select="."/>
```

```
</xsl:template>
<xsl:template match="/">

<html>
        <body>
                <xsl:apply-templates/>
        </body>
        </html>
    </xsl:template>
</xsl:stylesheet>
```

The XML file class.xml is linked to the XSLT code by adding the *xml-stylesheet* reference. The XSLT code then applies its *rules* to transform the XML document.

Before XSLT: classoriginal.xml

After XSLT rules are applied: class.xml

However, if you were to "view the source" of these XML files in your browser you would just see the XML document and not the transformed file. XSLT does not change an XML document, but this example shows how XSLT can be used to temporarily manipulate XML.

Below we have manually reconstructed the XSLT output that you see when you click class.xml. This HTML was created from an XML document bring transformed by our XSLT code.

XSLT Output (What you see in your browser):

```
<html>
<body>
        <p><b>Jack</b></p>
        <p><b>Harry</b></p>
        <p><b>Rebecca</b></p>
        <p><u>Mr. Bean</u></p>
</body>
</html>
```

As you can see, we used XSLT to convert the XML document into a simple webpage. Because we are an internet related web site all of our XSLT chapters will be focusing on browser ready XSLT output. However, you can pretty much do anything with XSLT!

XSLT Syntax

Now that you've seen one of the applications of XSLT, it's time to get into the nitty gritty details. The next few chapters will teach you the basics of XSLT, so that you can begin to write your own XML transformations with XSLT!

This chapter will teach you the basics of syntax and the necessary parts that must be in every XSLT file. Most of this information is just code that you can copy and paste to get started in XSLT.

If you would like to follow along, we recommend that you create a blank text file and save it as *class.xsl*. We will be adding to this file throughout the tutorial.

XSLT Declaration

This is more of a technicality, but you should include an XML declaration at the top of your XSLT documents. The attribute *version* defines what version of XML you are using.

XSLT Code (Work in Progress!):

```
<?xml version="1.0" ?>
```
XSLT - Stylesheet Root Element

Every XSLT file must have the root element *xsl:stylesheet*. This root element has two attributes that must be included:

- **version** - the version of XSLT
- **xmlns:xsl** - the XSLT namespace, which is a URI to w3.org

As you probably guessed, an XSLT file is a well-formed XML document.

XSLT Code

```
<?xml version="1.0" ?>
<xsl:stylesheet version= "1.0" xmlns:xsl=
    "http://www.w3.org/1999/XSL/Transform">
</xsl:stylesheet>
```

If you want to follow along on your own computer, copy and paste that text and save the file as *class.xsl*.

You do not need to know the intricacies of the *xsl:stylesheet* to use XSLT. What you do need to remember is to include both the XML declaration and the root element in your XSLT code!

XSL: Namespace Prefix

As you probably noticed, the root element specifies the XSL namespace. This basically means you have to put a **xsl:** prefix before every XSL element. Although this may seem annoying, it is absolutely required, so you better get used to it! The standard form of an XSL element is:

xsl:*element*

Syntax Overview

In this chapter you learned about the required pieces for valid XSLT code. You also learned that every XSLT element has an *xsl:* prefix to specify its namespace.

The rest of XSLT is just learning the special elements and attributes that XSLT uses. The next few chapters will talk about the most important XSLT elements and their related attributes.

Stylesheet Reference

This chapterwill teach you how to link your XML document to your XSLT stylesheet. This is the magic step that connects your XML to a XSLT file! If you do not follow the steps in this chapterto link your files, XSLT will not work properly.

xml-stylesheet

xml-stylesheet is a special declaration in XML for linking XML with stylesheets. Place this after your XML declaration to link your XML file to your XSLT code.

xml-stylesheet has two attributes:

1. **type**: the type of file being linked to. We will be using the value *text/xsl* to specify XSLT.

2. **href**: the location of the file. If you saved your XSLT and XML file in the same directory, you can simply use the XSLT filename.

If you have been following along with this tutorial, your XSLT file should be named class.xsl. Make sure that both your XSLT and XML file are in the same directory.

```xml
<?xml version="1.0" encoding="UTF-8"?>
<?xml-stylesheet type="text/xsl" href="class.xsl"?>
<class>
    <student>Jack</student>
    <student>Harry</student>
    <student>Rebecca</student>
    <teacher>Mr. Bean</teacher>
</class>
```

Save this XML file as class.xml and your XML file will be linked to your XSLT file. After you have finished this step you can continue learning XSLT!

xsl:template

The purpose of XSLT is to take an XML document and transform it into something new. To transform an XML document, XSLT must be able to do two things well:

1. Find information in the XML document

2. Add additional text and/or data. For example, in a previous example we added HTML tags.

Both of these items are taken care of with the very important XSL element *xsl:template*.

xsl:template Match Attribute

To find information in an XML document you will need to use xsl:template's *match* attribute. It is in this attribute that you use your knowledge of Path to find information in your XML document.

We will be using class.xml as our example XML document.

```xml
<?xml version="1.0" encoding="UTF-8"?>
<?xml-stylesheet type="text/xsl" href="class.xsl"?>
<class>
    <student>Jack</student>
    <student>Harry</student>
    <student>Rebecca</student>
    <teacher>Mr. Bean</teacher>
</class>
```

If we wanted to find *student* elements we would set the *match* attribute to a simple XPath expression: *student*.

Every time we find a student let's print something out. The text we want printed must go between the opening and closing tags of <xsl:template>. Let's have it print out "Found a learner!"

The following XSLT code will find *student* elements in the XML and output "Found a learner!" for each student element. This example displays both the *finding* and the *adding text* functionality of XSLT!

```
<?xml version="1.0" ?>
<xsl:stylesheet version="1.0" xmlns:xsl="http://www.w3.org/1999/XSL/Transform">
    <xsl:template match="student">
        Found a learner!
    </xsl:template>
</xsl:stylesheet>
```

This simple XSLT does not work in Firefox because the output is not well-formed XML. However, Internet Explorer 6.0+ will view it just fine. Here is the beginning of our XSLT transformation: class1.xml.

CHAPTER 8

Introduction XQuery

In this chapter, you will secure information.

You will:

- This chapter will introduce the XQuery technology and its role in SQL Server 2005.

- List the guidelines to be follow in order to implement best practices.

What is XQuery?

The best way to explain XQuery is to say that XQuery is to XML what SQL is to database tables. XQuery is designed to query XML data - not just XML files, but anything that can appear as XML, including databases.

XQuery specification, were released in the winter of 2002. Since than XQuery has become a powerful and convenient language designed for processing XML data. That means not only files in XML format, but as I said before it also processes other data including databases whose structure (nested, named trees with attributes) is similar to XML.

XQuery is an interesting language with some unusual ideas. This chapter provides a high level view of XQuery, introducing the main ideas you should understand before you go deeper or actually try to use it.

What You Should Already Know

Before you continue you by now you should have a basic understanding of the following:

- HTML / XHTML
- XML / XML Namespaces
- XPath

If you still have problems understanding these concepts I encourage to re-read the chapters leading here. If you want to study these subjects first, we encourage completing the labs found at the end of each chapter; this will help establish a foundation for this topic.

Now that we establish some pre-requisites lets continue with our chapter.

What is XQuery?

Previously we made the statement that XQuery is design to part XML Data specially that which resided in the Database, such as SQL Server 2005 and Oracle 11g. The XQuery is composes of five main facts:

- XQuery is **the** language for querying XML data
- XQuery for XML is like SQL for databases
- XQuery is built on XPath expressions

- XQuery is supported by all the major database engines (IBM, Oracle, Microsoft, etc.)
- XQuery is a W3C Recommendation

The database community has long been looking for a richer data model that will enable data interchange, specifically for:

- hierarchical databases
- object-oriented databases
- multi-dimensional databases but no consensus has emerged yet.

XML querying offers features which allows you the end user or administrator to create a rich interaction between system in multiple heterogeneous environments, therefore XQuery is relevant for:

- **human-readable documents**
  to retrieve individual documents, to provide dynamic indexes, to perform context-sensitive searching, and to generate new documents
- **data-oriented documents**
  to query (virtual) XML representations of databases, to transform data into new XML representations, and to integrate data from multiple heterogeneous data sources
- **mixed-model documents**
  to perform queries on documents with embedded data, such as catalogs, patient health records, employment records, or business analysis documents

XQuery and XML

XQuery is a language for finding and extracting elements and attributes from XML documents. Later on I will refer to the XQuery Language as an Expression Language; that very statement personifies the role of XQuery in a development environment. For this reason the W3C consortium query working Group identified many technical requirements:

- at least one **XML syntax** (at least one human-readable syntax)
- must be **declarative**

- must be protocol independent
- must respect XML data model
- must be **namespace aware**
- must **coordinate with XML Schema**
- must work even if schemas are unavailable
- must support simple and complex datatypes
- must support **universal and existential quantifiers**
- must support operations on hierarchy and sequence of document structures
- must **combine information from multiple documents**
- must support aggregation
- must be **able to transform and to create XML structures**
- must be able to traverse ID references

In short, it must be SQL generalized to XML! In order to be true XQuery compatible. It is derived from several previous proposals:

- XML-QL
- YATL
- Lorel
- Quilt

It is this diverse background which creates XQuery fundamental principles of performance. XQuery relies on XPath and XML Schema datatypes XQuery is **not** an XML language - a version in XML syntax is called XQueryX

XQuery Defined

A **query** in XQuery is an expression that:

- reads a sequence of XML fragments or atomic values
- returns a sequence of XML fragments or atomic values

The **principal forms** of XQuery expressions are:

- path expressions
- element constructors

- FLWOR ("flower") expressions
- list expressions
- conditional expressions
- quantified expressions
- datatype expressions

Expressions are evaluated relative to a **context**:

- namespaces
- variables
- functions
- date and time
- context item (current node or atomic value)
- context position (in the sequence being processed)
- context size (of the sequence being processed)

The simplest kind of query is just an **XPath 2.0** expression.

An Expression Language

The first thing to note is that in XQuery everything is an expression which evaluates to a value. An XQuery program or script is a just an expression, together with some optional function and other definitions. So 3+4 is a complete, valid XQuery program which evaluates to the integer 7.

There are no side-effects or updates in the XQuery standard, though they will probably be added at a future date. The standard specifies the *result value* of an expression or program, but it does not specify *how* it is to be evaluated. An implementation has considerable freedom in how it evaluates an XQuery program, and what optimizations it does.

> **if (3 < 4) then "yes!" else "no!"**

You can define local variable definitions using a let-expression:

> **let $x := 5 let $y := 6 return 10*$x+$y**

This evaluates to 56.

As you can see above there are many ways in which we can declare expressions in XQuery, since XQuery by design is an Expression based Language. Another simple path expression looks like:

document("recipes.xml")//recipe[title="Ricotta Pie"]//ingredient[@amount]

- the result is all simple ingredients used to prepare Ricotta Pie in the recipe collection
- the result is given as a list of XML fragments, each rooted with an **ingredient** element
- the **order** of the fragments respects the document order (order matters! - as opposed to SQL)

The initial context for the path expression is given by **document("recipes.xml")** (similarly to **XPointer**).

Some XQuery specific extension of XPath:

- location steps may follow a new **IDREF axis**
- an arbitrary XQuery expression may be used as a location step

XQuery Conditional Expressions

"If-Then-Else" expressions are allowed in XQuery.

Example:

```
for $x in doc("books.xml")/bookstore/book
returnif ($x/@category="CHILDREN")
then <name>{data($x/title)}</child>
else <adult>{data($x/title)}</adult>
```

Notes on the "if-then-else" syntax: parentheses around the if expression are required. else is required, but it can be just else ().

The result:

```
<adult>Everyday Italian</adult>
<child>Harry Potter</child>
<adult>Learning XML</adult>
<adult>XQuery Kick Start</adult>
```

Self Evaluation

An XQuery expression may construct a new XML element:

```
<employee empid="12345">
    <name>John Doe</name>
    <job>XML specialist</job>
    <deptno>187</deptno>
    <salary>125000</salary>
</employee>
```

which just evaluates to itself.

In the XQuery syntax this is unambiguous - XQueryX must use namespaces!

More interestingly, an expression may use values bound to variables:

```
<employee empid="{$id}">
 <name>{$name}</name>
 {$job}
 <deptno>{$deptno}</deptno>
 <salary>{$SGMLspecialist+100000}</salary>
</employee>
```

Here the variables $id, $name, and $job must be bound to appropriate XML fragments or strings.

XQuery Comparisons

In XQuery there are two ways of comparing values.

1. General comparisons: =, !=, <, <=, >, >=
2. Value comparisons: eq, ne, lt, le, gt, ge

The difference between the two comparisons methods are shown below.

XQuery expressions:

$bookstore//book/@q > 10
The expression above returns true if any q attributes

have values greater than 10.
$bookstore//book/@q gt 10

The expression above returns true if there is only one q attribute returned by the expression, and its value is greater than 10. If more than one q is returned, an error occurs.Primitive Data Types

The primitive's data types in XQuery are the same as for XML Schema.

- Numbers, including integers and floating-point numbers.

- The boolean values true and false.

- Strings of characters, for example: "Hello world!". These are immutable - i.e. you cannot modify a character in a string.

- Various types to represent dates, times, and durations.

- A few XML-related types. For example a *QName* is a pair of a local name (like template) and a URL, which is used to represent a tag name like xsl:template after it has been namespace-resolved.

Derived types are variations or restrictions of other types. Primitive types and the types derived from them are known as *atomic types*, because an atomic value does not contain other values. Thus a string is considered atomic because XQuery does not have character values.

Node Values and Expressions

XQuery also has the necessary data types needed to represent XML values. It does this using *node* values, of which there are 7 kinds: element, attribute, namespace, text, comment, processing-instruction, and document (root) nodes. These are very similar to the corresponding DOM classes such as Node, Element and so on. Some XQuery implementations use DOM objects to implement node values, though implementations may use other representations.

Various standard XQuery functions create or return nodes. The document function reads an XML file specified by a URL argument and returns a document root node. (The root element is a child of the root node.)

You can also create new node objects directly in the program. The most convenient way to do that is to use an *element constructor* expression, which looks just like regular XML data:

```
<p>See <a href="index.html"><i>here</i></a> for info.</p>
```

You can use *{curly braces}* to embed XQuery expression inside element constructors. Thus,

```
let $i := 2 return
let $r := <em>Value </em> return
 <p>{$r} of 10*{$i} is {10*$i}.</p>
```

Creates

```
<p><em>Value </em> of 10*2 is 20.</p>
```

Popular *template processors*, like JSP, ASP, and PHP, allow you to embed expressions in a programming language into HTML content. XQuery gives you that ability, plus the ability to embed XML/HTML forms inside expressions, and to have them be the value of variables and parameters.

XQuery node values are immutable (you cannot modify a node after it has been created).

Sequences

We've seen atomic values (numbers, strings, etc), and node values (elements, attributes, etc). These are together known as *simple values*. XQuery expressions actually evaluate to *sequences* of simple values. The comma operator can be used to concatenate two values or sequences. For example,

3,4,5

is a sequence consisting of 3 integers. Note that a sequence containing just single value is the same as that value by itself. You cannot nest sequences. To illustrate this, we'll use the count function, which takes one argument and returns the number of values in that sequence. So the expression

```
let $a := 3,4
let $b := ($a, $a)
let $c := 99
let $d := ()
return (count($a), count($b), count($c), count($d))
evaluates to (2, 4, 1, 0) because $b is the same as (3,4,3,4).
```

Many of the standard functions for working with nodes return sequences. The children function returns a sequence of the child nodes of the argument. Thus,

> **children(<p>This is very cool.</p>)**
> **returns this sequence of 3 values:**
> **"This is ", very, " cool."**

Path Expressions and Relationship to XPath

XQuery borrows *path expressions* from XPath. XQuery can be viewed as a generalization of XPath. Except for some obscure forms (mostly unusual "axis specifiers"), all XPath expressions are also XQuery expressions. For this reason the XPath specification is also being revised by the XQuery committee, with the plan that XQuery 1.0 and XPath 2.0 will be released about the same time.

The following simple example assumes an XML file "mybook.xml" whose root element is a <book>, containing some <chapter> children:

> **let $book := document("mybook.xml")/book**
> **return $book/chapter**

The document function returns the root node of a document. The /book expression selects the child elements of the root that are named book, so $book gets set to the single root element.

The $book/chapter selects the child elements of the top-level book elements, which results in a sequence of the second-level chapter nodes in *document order*.

Predicate Example:

> **$book//para[@class="warning"]**

The double slash is a convenience syntax to select all descendants (rather than just children) of $book, selecting only <para> element nodes that have an attribute node named class whose value is "warning"

One difference to note between XPath and XQuery is that XPath expressions may return a *node set*, whereas the same XQuery expression will return a node sequence. For compatibility these sequences will be in *document order* and with duplicates removed, which makes them equivalent to sets.

SQL Server Supporting Technology

XSLT is very useful for expressing very simple transformations, but more complicated stylesheets (especially anything with non-trivial logic or programming) can often be written more concisely using XQuery.

Iterating Over Sequences

A for expression lets you "loop" over the elements of a sequence:

> **for $x in (1 to 3) return ($x,10+$x)**

The for expression first evaluates the expression following the in. Then for each value of the resulting sequence, the variable (in this case $x) is bound to the value, and the return expression evaluated using that variable binding. The value of the entire for expression is the concatenation of all values of the return expression, in order. So the example evaluates to this 6-element sequence: 1,11,2,12,3,13.

Here is a more useful example. Assume again that mybook.xml is a <book> that contains some <chapter> elements. Each <chapter> has a <title>. The following will create a simple page that lists the titles:

```
<html>{
  let $book := document("mybook.xml")/book
  for $ch in $book/chapter
    return <h2>{$ch/title)</h2>
}</html>
```

The term "FLWR expressions" includes both for and let expressions. The acronym FLWR refers to the fact that it consists of one or more for and/or let clauses, an optional where clause, and a result clause. A where clause causes the result clause to be evaluated only when the where where expression is true.

The next example has a nested loop, allowing us to combine two sequences: one of customer elements and the other of order elements. We want to find the name(s) of customers who have ordered the part whose part_id is "xx".

```
for $c in customers
for $o in orders
where $c.cust_id=$o.cust_id and $o.part_id="xx"
return $c.name
```

This is essentially a *join* of two *tables* as commonly performed using relational databases. An important goal for XQuery is that it should be usable as a query language for XML databases. Compare the corresponding SQL statement,

```
select customers.name
from customers, orders
where customers.cust_id=orders.cust_id
and orders.part_id="xx"
```

XQuery Functions

XQuery includes over 100 built-in functions. There are functions for string values, numeric values, date and time comparison, node and QName manipulation, sequence manipulation, Boolean values, and more. You can also define your own functions in XQuery.

The default prefix for the function namespace is fn:.

XQuery wouldn't be much of a programming language without user-defined functions. Such function definitions appear in the *query prologue* of an XQuery program. It's worth noting that function parameters and function results can be primitive values, nodes, or sequences of either.

The following is a recursive utility function. It returns all the descendant nodes of the argument, including the argument node itself. It does a depth-first traversal of the argument, returning the argument, and then looping over the argument node's children, recursively calling itself for each child.

```
define function descendant-or-self ($x)
{
  $x,
  for $y in children($x)
    return descendant-or-self($y)
}
descendant-or-self(<a>X<b>Y</b></a>)
Which evaluates to this sequence of length 4:
<a>X<b>Y</b></a>; "X"; <b>Y</b>; "Y"
```

A call to a function can appear where an expression may appear. Look at the examples below:

Example 1: In an element

<name>{uppercase($booktitle)}</name>

Example 2: In the predicate of a path expression

doc("books.xml")/bookstore/book[substring(title,1,5)='Harry']

Example 3: In a let clause

let $name := (substring($booktitle,1,4))

XQuery User-Defined Functions

If you cannot find the XQuery function you need, you can write your own. User-defined functions can be defined in the query or in a separate library.

Syntax

```
declare function prefix:function_name($parameter AS datatype)
  AS returnDatatype
{
(: ...function code here... :)
};
```

Guide for user-defined functions:

- Use the declare function keyword
- The name of the function must be prefixed
- The data type of the parameters are mostly the same as the data types defined in XML Schema
- The body of the function must be surrounded by curly braces

Example of a User-defined Function Declared in the Query

```
declare function local:minPrice(
  $price as xs:decimal?,
  $discount as xs:decimal?)
  AS xs:decimal?
{
let $disc := ($price * $discount) div 100
return ($price - $disc)
};
(: Below is an example of how to call the function above :)
<minPrice>{local:minPrice($book/price,
$book/discount)}</minPrice>
```

Sorting and Context

If you want to sort a sequence you can use a sortby expression. To sort a sequence of books in order of author name you can do:

$books sortby (author/name)

The sortby takes an input sequence (in this case $books) and one or more *ordering expressions*. During sorting the implementation needs to compare two values from the input sequence to determine which comes first. It does that by evaluating the ordering expression(s) in the *context* of a value from the input sequence. So the path expression author/name is evaluated many times, each time relative to a different book as the *context (or current) item*.

Path expressions also use and set the context. In author/name the name children that are returned are those of the context item, which is an author item.

Type Specification

XQuery is a strongly typed programming language. Like Java and C#, for example, it's a mix of static typing (type consistency checked at compile-time) and dynamic typing (run-time type tests). However, the types in XQuery are different from the classes familiar from object-oriented programming. Instead, it has types to match XQuery's data model, and it allows you to import types form XML Schema.

```
if ($child instance of element section)
then process-section($child)
else ( ) {--nothing--}
```

This invokes the process-section function if the value of $child is an element whose tag name is section. XQuery has a convenient typeswitch shorthand for matching a value against a number of types. The following converts a set of tag names to a different set.

```
define function convert($x) {
  typeswitch ($x)
    case element para return <p>{process-children($x)}</p>
    case element emph  return <em>{process-children($x)}</em>
    default return process-children($x)
}
define function process-children($x) {
  for $ch in children($x) return convert($ch)
```

}
Adding Elements and Attributes to the Result

As we have seen in a previous chapter, we may include elements and attributes from the input document ("books.xml) in the result:

```
for $x in doc("books.xml")/bookstore/book/title
order by $x
return $x
```

The XQuery expression above will include both the title element and the lang attribute in the result, like this:

```
<title lang="en">Everyday Italian</title>
<title lang="en">Harry Potter</title>
<title lang="en">Learning XML</title>
<title lang="en">XQuery Kick Start</title>
```

The XQuery expression above returns the title elements the exact same way as they are described in the input document.

We now want to add our own elements and attributes to the result!

Add HTML Elements and Text

Now, we want to add some HTML elements to the result. We will put the result in an HTML list - together with some text:

```
<html>
<body>
<h1>Bookstore</h1>
<ul>
{
for $x in doc("books.xml")/bookstore/book
order by $x/title
return <li>{data($x/title)}. Category: {data($x/@category)}</li>
}
</ul>
</body>
</html>
```

The XQuery expression above will generate the following result:

```
<html>
<body>
<h1>Bookstore</h1>
<ul>
<li>Everyday Italian. Category: COOKING</li>
<li>Harry Potter. Category: CHILDREN</li>
<li>Learning XML. Category: WEB</li>
<li>XQuery Kick Start. Category: WEB</li>
</ul>
</body>
</html>
```

Add Attributes to HTML Elements

Next, we want to use the category attribute as a class attribute in the HTML list:

```
<html>
<body>
<h1>Bookstore</h1>
<ul>
{
for $x in doc("books.xml")/bookstore/book
order by $x/title
return <li class="{data($x/@category)}">{data($x/title)}</li>
}
</ul>
</body>
</html>
```

The XQuery expression above will generate the following result:

```
<html>
<body>
<h1>Bookstore</h1>
<ul>
<li class="COOKING">Everyday Italian</li>
<li class="CHILDREN">Harry Potter</li>
```

```
<li class="WEB">Learning XML</li>
<li class="WEB">XQuery Kick Start</li>
</ul>
</body>
</html>
```

Selecting and Filtering Elements

As we have seen in the previous chapters, we are selecting and filtering elements with either a Path expression or with a FLWOR expression.

Look at the following FLWOR expression:

```
for $x in doc("books.xml")/bookstore/book
where $x/price>30
order by $x/title
return $x/title
```

- for - (optional) binds a variable to each item returned by the in expression
- let - (optional)
- where - (optional) specifies a criteria
- order by - (optional) specifies the sort-order of the result
- return - specifies what to return in the result

The for Clause

The for clause binds a variable to each item returned by the in expression. The for clause results in iteration. There can be multiple for clauses in the same FLWOR expression.

To loop a specific number of times in a for clause, you may use the **to** keyword:

```
for $x in (1 to 5)
return <test>{$x}</test>
```

Result:

```
<test>1</test>
<test>2</test>
<test>3</test>
```

```
<test>4</test>
<test>5</test>
```

The **at** keyword can be used to count the iteration:

```
for $x at $i in doc("books.xml")/bookstore/book/title
return <book>{$i}. {data($x)}</book>
```

Result:

```
<book>1. Everyday Italian</book>
<book>2. Harry Potter</book>
<book>3. XQuery Kick Start</book>
<book>4. Learning XML</book>
```

It is also allowed with more than one in expression in the for clause. Use comma to separate each in expression:

```
for $x in (10,20), $y in (100,200)
return <test>x={$x} and y={$y}</test>
```

Result:

```
<test>x=10 and y=100</test>
<test>x=10 and y=200</test>
<test>x=20 and y=100</test>
<test>x=20 and y=200</test>
```

The let Clause

The let clause allows variable assignments and it avoids repeating the same expression many times. The let clause does not result in iteration.

```
let $x := (1 to 5)
return <test>{$x}</test>
```

Result:

```
<test>1 2 3 4 5</test>
```

The where Clause

The where clause is used to specify one or more criteria for the result:

> **where $x/price>30 and $x/price<100**

The order by Clause

The order by clause is used to specify the sort order of the result. Here we want to order the result by category and title:

> **for $x in doc("books.xml")/bookstore/book**
> **order by $x/@category, $x/title**
> **return $x/title**

Result:

> `<title lang="en">Harry Potter</title>`
> `<title lang="en">Everyday Italian</title>`
> `<title lang="en">Learning XML</title>`
> `<title lang="en">XQuery Kick Start</title>`

The return Clause

The return clause specifies what is to be returned.

> **for $x in doc("books.xml")/bookstore/book**
> **return $x/title**

Result:

> `<title lang="en">Everyday Italian</title>`
> `<title lang="en">Harry Potter</title>`
> `<title lang="en">XQuery Kick Start</title>`
> `<title lang="en">Learning XML</title>`

FLWOR expressions

The main engine of XQuery is the FLWOR expression:

- For-Let-Where-Order-Return
- pronounced "flower"
- generalizes SELECT-FROM-HAVING-WHERE from SQL

A complete example is: for $d in document("depts.xml")//deptno

```
let $e := document("emps.xml")//employee[deptno = $d]
where count($e) >= 10
order by avg($e/salary) descending
return
  <big-dept>
    { $d,
      <headcount>{count($e)}</headcount>,
      <avgsal>{avg($e/salary)}</avgsal>
    }
  </big-dept>
```

for generates an ordered list of bindings of deptno values to $d

- let associates to each binding a further binding of the list of emp elements with that department number to $e
- at this stage, we have an ordered list of tuples of bindings: ($d,$e)
- where filters that list to retain only the desired tuples
- order sorts that list by the given criteria
- return constructs for each tuple a resulting value

The combined result is in this case a list of departments with at least 10 employees, sorted by average salaries.

General Guidelines:

- for and let may be used many times in any order
- only one where is allowed
- many different sorting criteria can be specified

Note: the difference between for and let: for $x in /company/employee generates a list of bindings of $x to each employee element in the company, but:

let $x := /company/employee

generates a single binding of $x to the list of employee elements in the company.

This is also sufficient to compute joins of documents: for $p IN document("www.irs.gov/taxpayers.xml")//person

```
        for $n IN document("neighbors.xml")//neighbor[ssn = $p/ssn]
return
 <person>
  <ssn> { $p/ssn } </ssn>
  { $n/name }
  <income> { $p/income } </income>
 </person>
```

Things not covered here:

- hundreds of built-in operators and functions - contains anything you might think of
- computed element and attribute names - allow more flexible queries
- user-defined functions - allow general-purpose computations
- views and updates are still under development

XML databases

XML databases running XQuery may be:

- **native** - specialized engines evaluating queries on XML documents examples are Galax and Qexo
- **relational** - built on top of existing database engines most commercial database products support some version of this with a subset of XQuery or XPath

Native XML processing is:

- lightweight and easy to extend with new XML features
- unable to scale and weak on security, concurrency, transactions, recovery, ...

Relational XML processing is:

- an attempt to get the best from both worlds

XML Shredding

With relational processing, the XML document must be stored in a relation.

Mapping from XML to relations is called **shredding**, which for the recipes could look like:

Collection

id	Description
147	Some recipes used in the XML tutorial.

Recipe

id	parent	Title
231	147	Beef Parmesan with Garlic Angel Hair Pasta
237	147	Ricotta Pie
242	147	Linguine Pescadoro
247	147	Zuppa Inglese
253	147	Cailles en Sarcophages

Ingredient

id	Parent	name	amount	unit
411	231	beef cube steak	1.5	pound
462	237	ricotta cheese	3	pound
535	247	egg yolks	4	
612	247	pastry		
789	612	flour	3	cup
...	...	...	...	...

Preparation

id	parent

376	231
...	...

Step

id	parent	Text
423	376	Preheat oven to 350 degrees F (175 degrees C).
...	...	...

Comment

id	parent	Text
...	...	...

Nutrition

id	parent	calories	fat	carbohydrates	protein	alcohol
...	...	...	...	...	...	...

In this construction, we have:

- one relation for each element type
- a unique id for each occurrence of an element
- identifications of the parent nodes
- the ids of siblings are ordered

From XQuery to SQL

Using a tool like Visual Studio.Net, SQL Server Management Studio, XQuery queries can be translated into equivalent SQL queries.

As a simple example, the following XQuery query:

```
//ingredient[@name="butter"]/@amount
```

corresponds to the simple SQL query:

select ingredient.amount

from ingredient

where ingredient.name='butter'

This becomes much more complicated for general queries. The performance of a translated query depends on the shredding. In response, the system performs **adaptive** shredding.

Mixed processing

Mixed processing creates an spectrum of possibilities between native and relational XML databases.

Shredding with fine XML fragments:

- small irregular XML fragments are stored as character data in tuples (**VARCHAR**)
- simplifies the mapping
- may improve performance
- example: XHTML help texts

Shredding with coarse XML fragments:

- larger XML fragments are stored as external character data (**CLOB**)
- necessary if the schema is unknown or some XML features are not supported
- decreases performance
- example: SOAP message contents

CHAPTER 9

Introduction XPath

In this chapter, you will learn to.

- List the steps to be taken to protect information from unauthorized access.
- List the guidelines to be followed to prevent a virus attack.

SQL Server Supporting Technology

What is XPath?

As you know, XML was created to be a self-describing markup format. As XML matured, new XML related creations were popping up. Although you could create a nicely structured document with XML, there didn't seem to be an easy way to find information inside the document.

XPath is a language for finding information in an XML document. XPath is used to navigate through elements and attributes in an XML document.

XPath is a major element in the W3C's XSLT standard - and XQuery and XPointer are both built on XPath expressions. So an understanding of XPath is fundamental to a lot of advanced XML usage. XPath is a language for finding information in an XML document. XPath is used to navigate through elements and attributes in an XML document. XPath became a W3C Recommendation 16. November 1999.

It was designed to be used by XSLT, XPointer and other XML parsing software.

What You Should Already Know

Before you start our XPath chapter you should have a strong understanding of XML. If you skipped the XML chapters, now would be a good time to read it! You will not be able to fully understand XPath if your knowledge of XML is lacking. You should have a basic understanding of the following

- HTML / XHTML
- XML / XML Namespaces
- Schema's
- Namesspaces
- XSLT

XML documents can be thought of as a Tree Structure – as we discussed in the previous chapters - made up of parent, child, and sibling relationships.

Because of this very logical layout of an XML document it seems like there should be a standard way to find information.

XPath - Finding Information

XPath is the solution to finding information in an XML document. XPath uses expressions to find elements, attributes, and other information in your XML. If you had an XML document that contained a bunch of your favorite books, each with author children elements, you could use a one line XPath expression to find all the authors of your favorite books!

If you are thinking seriously about learning XML and its important related technologies, XPath is one area you can't pass up!

XPath - Used in XSLT

The most common place people might see XPath expressions are in XSLT(Extensible Stylesheet Language Transformation). We will be teaching XSLT after we have taught you the steppingstone knowledge of XPath.

XPointer and XQuery are both new XML related technologies that extend or borrow from XPath. XPath truly is a keystone for XML related learning!

What is XPath?

XPath is a syntax for defining parts of an XML document

- XPath uses path expressions to navigate in XML documents
- XPath contains a library of standard functions
- XPath is a major element in XSLT
- XPath is a W3C Standard

XPath Path Expressions

XPath uses path expressions to select nodes or node-sets in an XML document. These path expressions look very much like the expressions you see when you work with a traditional computer file system.

XPath Standard Functions

XPath includes over 100 built-in functions. There are functions for string values, numeric values, date and time comparison, node and QName manipulation, sequence manipulation, Boolean values, and more.

XPath is Used in XSLT

XPath is a major element in the XSLT standard. Without XPath knowledge you will not be able to create XSLT documents.

> **Note:** You can read more about XSLT in next chapter.

XQuery and XPointer are both built on XPath expressions. XQuery 1.0 and XPath 2.0 share the same data model and support the same functions and operators.

There are seven kinds of nodes within the XPath tree structure: element, attribute, text, namespace, processing-instruction, comment, and document (root) nodes.

We will take a detail look at each of this structures this will help you understand the role of XPath in relation to later topics such as XQuery. First lets look at the nodes in the tree.

XPath - Element

The most common usage of XPath is used to select *elements* in an XML document. This chapter will provide a walkthrough of selecting many different elements, at different levels, in the XML Tree.

XPath Terminology

As we said before XPath, has seven kinds of nodes: element, attribute, text, namespace, processing-instruction, comment, and document (root) nodes. XML documents are treated as trees of nodes. The root of the tree is called the document node (or root node).

Look at the following XML document:

```xml
<?xml version="1.0" encoding="ISO-8859-1"?>
<bookstore>
    <book>
      <title lang="en">Harry Potter</title>
      <author>J K. Rowling</author>
      <year>2005</year>
      <price>29.99</price>
    </book>
</bookstore>
```

Example of nodes in the XML document above:

```
<bookstore>  (document node)
<author>J K. Rowling</author>  (element node)
lang="en"  (attribute node)
```

Atomic values

Atomic values are nodes with no children or parent.

Example of atomic values:

> R. Garcia PhD
> "en"

Items

Items are atomic values or nodes.

Relationship of Nodes

Each element and attribute has one parent.

In the following example; the book element is the parent of the title, author, year, and price:

```
<book>
    <title>Introduction to Oracle 10g</title>
    <author>Rigoberto Garcia PhD</author>
    <year>2005</year>
    <price>69.99</price>
</book>
```

Children

If we wanted to select the *title* of *author* we would have to make an even longer path of elements to reach our final destination. Element nodes may have zero, one or more children.

In the following example; the title, author, year, and price elements are all children of the book element:

```
<book>
    <title>Introduction to Oracle 10g</title>
    <author>Rigoberto Garcia PhD</author>
```

Siblings

Nodes that have the same parent.

In the following example; the title, author, year, and price elements are all siblings:

```
<book>
    <title>Introduction to Oracle 10g</title>
    <author>Rigoberto Garcia PhD</author>
    <year>2005</year>
    <price>69.99</price>
</book>
```

Ancestors

A node's parent, parent's parent, etc.

In the following example; the ancestors of the title element are the book element and the bookstore element:

```
<bookstore>
    <book>
        <title>Introduction to Oracle 10g</title>
        <author>Rigoberto Garcia PhD</author>
        <year>2005</year>
        <price>69.99</price>
    </book>
<bookstore>
```

Descendants

A node's children, children's children, etc.

In the following example; descendants of the bookstore element are the book, title, author, year, and price elements:

```
<bookstore>
    <book>
        <title>Introduction to Oracle 10g</title>
        <author>Rigoberto Garcia PhD</author>
        <year>2005</year>
        <price>69.99</price>
    </book>
<bookstore>
```

XML Example

We will use the following XML document in the examples below.

```
<?xml version="1.0" encoding="ISO-8859-1"?>

<bookstore>
    <book>
        <title>Introduction to Oracle 10g</title>
        <author>Rigoberto Garcia PhD</author>
        <year>2005</year>
        <price>69.99</price>
    </book>
    <book>
        <title>Our family Poetry</title>
        <author>Rigoberto Garcia PhD</author>
        <year>2006</year>
        <price>29.95</price>
    </book>
<bookstore>
```

Relative Location

Expressions that use *relative location paths* open up a whole new set of options for you. You can do things like select **every** *year* element in an XML document.

To construct an XPath expression to select every *year* element, we only need to type one word.

XPath Expression:

year

This piece of XPath will select all of the *year* elements in our *Bookstore* XML document. If you were trying to find the total items in stock this type of XPath expression would be perfect!

Selecting Nodes

XPath uses path expressions to select nodes in an XML document. The node is selected by following a path or steps. The most useful path expressions are listed below:

Expression	Description
nodename	Selects all child nodes of the node
/	Selects from the root node
//	Selects nodes in the document from the current node that match the selection no matter where they are
.	Selects the current node
..	Selects the parent of the current node
@	Selects attributes

Examples

In the table below we have listed some path expressions and the result of the expressions:

Path Expression	*Result*
Bookstore	*Selects all the child nodes of the bookstore element*
/bookstore	*Selects the root element bookstore* **Note:** *If the path starts with a slash (/) it always represents an absolute path to an element!*
bookstore/book	*Selects all book elements that are children of bookstore*
//book	*Selects all book elements no matter where they are in the document*
bookstore//book	*Selects all book elements that are descendant of the bookstore element, no matter where they are under the bookstore element*
//@lang	*Selects all attributes that are named lang*

SQL Server Supporting Technology

Predicates

Predicates are used to find a specific node or a node that contains a specific value.

Predicates are always embedded in square brackets.

Examples

In the table below we have listed some path expressions with predicates and the result of the expressions:

Path Expression	Result
/bookstore/book[0]	Selects the first book element that is the child of the bookstore element. **Note:** IE5 and later has implemented that [0] should be the first node, but according to the W3C standard it should have been [1]!!
/bookstore/book[last()]	Selects the last book element that is the child of the bookstore element
/bookstore/book[last()-1]	Selects the last but one book element that is the child of the bookstore element
/bookstore/book[position()<3]	Selects the first two book elements that are children of the bookstore element
//title[@lang]	Selects all the title elements that have an attribute named lang
//title[@lang='eng']	Selects all the title elements that have an attribute named lang with a value of 'eng'
/bookstore/book[price>35.00]	Selects all the book elements of the bookstore element that have a price element with a value greater than 35.00
/bookstore/book[price>35.00]/title	Selects all the title elements of the book

	elements of the bookstore element that have a price element with a value greater than 35.00

Selecting Unknown Nodes

XPath wildcards can be used to select unknown XML elements.

Wildcard	Description
*	Matches any element node
@*	Matches any attribute node
node()	Matches any node of any kind

Examples

In the table below we have listed some path expressions and the result of the expressions:

Path Expression	Result
/bookstore/*	Selects all the child nodes of the bookstore element
//*	Selects all elements in the document
//title[@*]	Selects all title elements which have any attribute

Selecting Several Paths

By using the | operator in an XPath expression you can select several paths.

Examples

In the table below we have listed some path expressions and the result of the expressions:

Path Expression	Result
//book/title | //book/price	Selects all the title AND price elements of all book elements
//title | //price	Selects all the title AND price elements in the document
/bookstore/book/title | //price	Selects all the title elements of the book element of the bookstore element AND all the price elements in the document

XML Example

We will use the following XML document in the examples below.

```
<?xml version="1.0" encoding="ISO-8859-1"?>

<bookstore>
    <book>
            <title>Introduction to Oracle 10g</title>
            <author>Rigoberto Garcia PhD</author>
            <year>2005</year>
            <price>69.99</price>
    </book>
    <book>
            <title>Our family Poetry</title>
            <author>Rigoberto Garcia PhD</author>
            <year>2006</year>
            <price>29.95</price>
    </book>
<bookstore>
```

XPath Axes

An axis defines a node-set relative to the current node.

AxisName	Result
ancestor	Selects all ancestors (parent, grandparent, etc.) of the current node
ancestor-or-self	Selects all ancestors (parent, grandparent, etc.) of the current node and the current node itself
attribute	Selects all attributes of the current node
child	Selects all children of the current node
descendant	Selects all descendants (children, grandchildren, etc.) of the current node
descendant-or-self	Selects all descendants (children, grandchildren, etc.) of the current node and the current node itself
following	Selects everything in the document after the closing tag of the current node
following-sibling	Selects all siblings after the current node
namespace	Selects all namespace nodes of the current node
parent	Selects the parent of the current node
preceding	Selects everything in the document that is before the start tag of the current node
preceding-sibling	Selects all siblings before the current node
self	Selects the current node

Location Path Expression

A location path can be absolute or relative. XPath can locate any type of information in an XML document with one line of code. These one liners are referred to as "expressions" and every piece of XPath that you write will be an expression. Just to make it crystal clear, here's the definition of an expression as it relates to our usage.

> **Expression**: In programming, a line of source code that returns a value when executed. ~Computer Desktop Encyclopedia

An XPath expression is exactly that, it's a line of code that we use to get information from our XML document

A Simple XPath Expression

An XPath expression describes the location of an element or attribute in our XML document. By starting at the root element, we can select any element in the document by carefully creating a chain of children elements. Each element is separated by a slash "/".

An absolute location path starts with a slash (/) and a relative location path does not. In both cases the location path consists of one or more steps, each separated by a slash:

> **An absolute location path:**
> /step/step/...
> **A relative location path:**
> step/step/...

Each step is evaluated against the nodes in the current node-set.

A step consists of:

- an axis (defines the tree-relationship between the selected nodes and the current node)
- a node-test (identifies a node within an axis)
- zero or more predicates (to further refine the selected node-set)

The syntax for a location step is:

> **axisname::nodetest[predicate]**

Example	Result
child::book	Selects all book nodes that are children of the current node
attribute::lang	Selects the lang attribute of the current node
child::*	Selects all children of the current node

attribute::*	Selects all attributes of the current node
child::text()	Selects all text child nodes of the current node
child::node()	Selects all child nodes of the current node
descendant::book	Selects all book descendants of the current node
ancestor::book	Selects all book ancestors of the current node
ancestor-or-self::book	Selects all book ancestors of the current node - and the current as well if it is a book node
child::*/child::price	Selects all price grandchildren of the current node

An XPath expression returns either a node-set, a string, a Boolean, or a number.

XPath Operators

Below is a list of the operators that can be used in XPath expressions:

Operator	Description	Example	Return value
|	Computes two node-sets	//book | //cd	Returns a node-set with all book and cd elements
+	Addition	6 + 4	10
-	Subtraction	6 - 4	2
Div	**Division**	**8 div 4**	**2**
=	Equal	price=9.80	true if price is 9.80 false if price is 9.90
!=	Not equal	price!=9.80	true if price is 9.90 false if price is 9.80
<	Less than	price<9.80	true if price is 9.00

SQL Server Supporting Technology

			false if price is 9.80
<=	Less than or equal to	price<=9.80	true if price is 9.00 false if price is 9.90
>	Greater than	price>9.80	true if price is 9.90 false if price is 9.80
>=	Greater than or equal to	price>=9.80	true if price is 9.90 false if price is 9.70
or	or	price=9.80 or price=9.70	true if price is 9.80 false if price is 9.50
and	and	price>9.00 and price<9.90	true if price is 9.80 false if price is 8.50
*	Multiplication	6 * 4	24
mod	Modulus	5 mod 2	1

The XML Example Document

We will use the following XML document in the examples below.

"books.xml":

```
<?xml version="1.0" encoding="ISO-8859-1"?>

<bookstore>
    <book category="Computers">
        <title lang="en">Introduction to Oracle 10g</title>
        <author>Rigoberto Garcia PhD</author>
        <year>2005</year>
        <price>69.99</price>
    </book>
    <book category="Literature">
        <title lang="en">Our family Poetry</title>
        <author>Rigoberto Garcia PhD</author>
        <year>2006</year>
        <price>29.95</price>
    </book>
```

```
<bookstore>
```

Selecting Nodes

We will use the Microsoft XMLDOM object to load the XML document and the selectNodes() function to select nodes from the XML document:

```
set xmlDoc=CreateObject("Microsoft.XMLDOM")
xmlDoc.async="false"
xmlDoc.load("books.xml")
xmlDoc.selectNodes(path expression)
```

Select all book Nodes

The following example selects all the book nodes under the bookstore element:

```
xmlDoc.selectNodes("/bookstore/book")
```

Select the First book Node

The following example selects only the first book node under the bookstore element:

```
xmlDoc.selectNodes("/bookstore/book[0]")
```

Note: IE5 and later has implemented that [0] should be the first node, but according to the W3C standard it should have been [1]!!

A Workaround!

To solve the [0] and [1] problem in IE5+, you can set the Selection Language to XPath.

The following example selects only the first book node under the bookstore element:

```
xmlDoc.setProperty "SelectionLanguage", "XPath"
xmlDoc.selectNodes("/bookstore/book[1]")
```

Select the prices

The following example selects the text from all the price nodes:

SQL Server Supporting Technology

xmlDoc.selectNodes("/bookstore/book/price/text()")

Selecting price Nodes with Price > 35

The following example selects all the price nodes with a price higher than 35:

xmlDoc.selectNodes("/bookstore/book[price>35]/price")

Selecting title Nodes with Price > 35

The following example selects all the title nodes with a price higher than 35:

xmlDoc.selectNodes("/bookstore/book[price>35]/title")

XPath Summary

This chapter has taught you how to find information in an XML document.

You have learned how to use XPath to navigate through elements and attributes in an XML document. You have also learned how to use some of the standard functions that are built-in in XPath.

What's Next?

The next step is to learn about XSLT, XQuery, XLink, and XPointer. In the next chapter we will introduce you to XSLT and it role in the MS Framework.

Vertical Bar | (Pipe)

XPath makes use of the character "|" which we will be referring to as *pipe* from here on out. The pipe character is a way of combining two or more expressions into one. Depending on where you are using XPath, this ability to combine multiple expressions into one may be useful.

Although you probably won't use this feature very often, it is possible to combine as many expressions as you want with the pipe character. Here is an example that selects all of the children elements of *chips* using |

Combining Two Expressions with |

When you need to select multiple things with one expression, chances are you will have to use the pipe character. In our bookstore.xml document we might want to select the children of *chips* and the children of *pop*. To do this we would use the pipe character "|".

Combining XPath Expression:

inventory/book/title/* | inventory/category/computer/*

This expression combines two expressions into one and will select every element that matches either expression.

Combining XPath Expression:

authos/title | author/amount | author/category

CHAPTER 10

Improving XML Data Access Performance with SQL Server 2005

In this chapter, you will secure information.

You will:

- Extracting data from xml columns
- Comparing traditional XML data access approaches with XQuery
- Combining XQuery and XSL-T
- Updating the contents of xml columns
- Comparing traditional XML update techniques with XQuery

SQL Server Supporting Technology

Introduction

This is the second in a series of three chapters that look at how the latest version of Microsoft's enterprise-level database, **SQL Server 2005**, now offers great support and close integration with XML as a data persistence format.

This includes new ways to validate, store and query XML documents that are stored within the database. SQL Server 2005 provides native support for XML that can vastly improve application performance, while supporting robust and safe multi-user access to the data contained within the XML documents.

The topics we covered in the previous article were:

A brief overview of the way that SQL Server 2005 stores XML documents and schemas

- How SQL Server 2005 provides support for querying and manipulating XML documents

- A simple test application that allows you to experiment with XQuery

- Updating the contents of xml columns

- Comparing traditional XML update techniques with XQuery

- Using XQuery in a managed code stored procedure

Storing XML in a Database

Just because XML was originally conceived as a stream-based or a disk-based data persistence format doesn't mean that developers ignored their usual data stores. After all, an XML document is basically just a string of text characters, and so can be stored in a database using a char, varchar, or text type column.

Of course, this means that, when you want to use the XML, you have to read the complete document from the column. And if you want to edit and update it, you have to write the complete document back into the table again. If it's a large document, this can soak up network bandwidth, processing and server resources, and reduce application performance.

Another approach is to "shred" the document into its component parts and store each value from the document in a separate column. This has several advantages. One is that you can store each value in a column of the appropriate data type (int, varchar, datetime, etc.). This allows simple indexing of the document (something you can't easily do if you store the whole thing in a single column), and means that comparisons can be made based on the correct data type.

In other words, you can search for things like product IDs or names without having to extract the whole document and parse it each time. And you can select rows that meet specific conditions, such as dates in a particular range, by simply using a SQL WHERE clause on the appropriate column.

The problem with the "shredding" approach is the amount of developer effort required to build the data access code that performs all these tasks, including validating the document, extracting each value, and interfacing with the database to persist and extract values and complete documents as required.

As they say in TV commercials, "there has to be a better way!" The better way is, of course, to use a database such as SQL Server 2005 that provides all these features built into the core database engine.

XML in a SQL Server 05-08

In the previous article, we saw how SQL Server 2005 provides several features that make persisting and managing XML document much easier and more efficient than the traditional approaches we've just been discussing. The core features are:

- A dedicated column type named xml that can be used to store XML documents or fragments of XML

- The ability to register XML schemas with SQL Server 2005, and store schema information within the database

- Automatic validation of XML documents when a schema is present; and automatic shredding of the XML data to support efficient querying and updating of the content

- An implementation of a subset of the W3C XQuery language to provide this querying and update facility

SQL Server Supporting Technology

- Support for hosting the .NET Common Language Runtime (CLR) within SQL Server, which allows stored procedures that manipulate XML documents to be written in managed code

We described these features in the previous article, and provided a simple application that you can use to experiment with XQuery in SQL Server 2005. In this and the subsequent article, we'll use the techniques outlined above to demonstrate how you can save time and effort, and get better application performance, when using XML in SQL Server 2005.

Applications

As well as the XQuery Tester application described in the previous article, you can also use several other pages provided in the downloadable samples to see XQuery in action. The full list of these examples is:

- Reading XML Values the Traditional Way
- Using a Simple XQuery with an 'xml' Column
- Comparing the Traditional Way and XQuery
- Using Parameters with an XQuery
- Combining XQuery and XSL-T
- Modifying an 'xml' Column with XQuery
- Comparing Traditional and XQuery Updates
- Using a Managed Code Stored Procedure in SQL Server 2005

The samples require Beta 2 of version 2.0 of the .NET Framework and SQL Server 2005. There is a ~readme.txt file in the samples that explains how to install and run them on your machine. Every page contains a [view source] link that displays the source code, and - where applicable - any other files used by that example.

We won't be listing all of the code in this article, because much of it uses standard ASP.NET and ADO.NET techniques to create the pages and connect to the database. What we will concentrate on is how the examples exploit the new XML data management features in SQL Server 2005.

Many of the examples use an un-typed xml column so that the queries are easier to assimilate (no namespace declaration or prefixes are required). However, some processes (such as the modify method when replacing values in the XML) require a typed column, and so the script we provide creates two tables - one named Store with an un-typed xml column and one named StoreTyped with a typed xml column. You'll see both used in the examples.

Traditional XML Handling

Traditionally, developers who need to access values in an XML document stored in a database would read the complete document into an XML parser, and then navigate through the document to extract the values they need. The first example, *Reading XML Values the Traditional Way*" demonstrates this approach. It uses a SQL statement that extracts the contents of the xml column named Demographics, for a specified CustomerID value:

```
Dim sql_getbank As String = "SELECT Demographics FROM Store " _ &
"WHERE CustomerID = @CustomerID"
```

The page also uses an ASP.NET GridView control and a SqlDataSource control to display a list of customers, and selecting one executes a procedure named ShowBankName.

This procedure connects to the database, creates a command and adds a parameter for the CustomerID to it, then calls the ExecuteScaler method of the command to get the XML from the matching row in the database:

```
Sub ShowBankName(ByVal sender As Object, ByVal e As EventArgs)
    Dim sXML As String = String.Empty
    Using con As New SqlConnection(ConfigurationManager.ConnectionStrings _
            ("XMLTestConnectionString").ConnectionString)
    Dim cmd As New SqlCommand(sql_getbank, con)
    cmd.Parameters.Add(New SqlParameter("@CustomerID", _
            Int32.Parse(grid1.SelectedDataKey.Value)))
    Try
      con.Open()
      sXML = cmd.ExecuteScalar()
      con.Close()
    Catch ex As Exception
```

```
        lblMessage.Text = ex.Message
      End Try
    End Using
```

Now the code can check if an XML document is available, and if so load it into an XmlDocument instance and use the SelectSingleNode method to get a reference to the BankName element. The value of this element is in the first child node (a text node), so it can be extracted from the Value property of ChildNodes(0) and displayed in a Label control on the page:

```
    ...
    If sXML <> String.Empty Then
      Dim xd As New XmlDocument()
      xd.LoadXml(sXML)
      Dim xn As XmlNode =   xd.SelectSingleNode("//BankName")
      lblMessage.Text = "Bank name is: <b>" &   xn.ChildNodes(0).Value  & "</b>"

    Else

      lblMessage.Text = "Cannot find bank name"
    End If
  End Sub
```

Extracting a Value Using XQuery

The second example, *Using a Simple XQuery with an 'xml' Column*, achieves the same result as the preceding example, but by using an XQuery instead. The SQL query used this time calls the query method of the Demographics column to access the BankName node, and uses the XPath data function to extract just the value (the content of the BankName element):

```
    Dim sql_getbank As String = "SELECT
      Demographics.query('data(//BankName)') " _
    & "FROM Store WHERE CustomerID =   @CustomerID"
```

Executing this query simply returns the bank name as a String, and so the ShowBankName routine in this example - after opening the connection to the database and executing the query - simply displays the value that is returned:

SQL Server Supporting Technology

```
lblMessage.Text = "Bank name is: <b>" & cmd.ExecuteScalar() & "</b>"
```

As you can see, this makes the code much simpler and more compact, and has the added benefit of reducing network traffic between the database and the data access code. Figure 1 shows the two example pages we've just described.

Comparing XQuery Performance with the Traditional Approach

The third example we provide, *"Comparing the Traditional Way and XQuery"*, does much the same as the two examples you've just seen, but this time extracts and displays the customer name and bank name for all 700+ rows in the Store and StoreTyped tables.

It allows you to choose one of three ways to accomplish this - using the traditional approach, using XQuery against an un-typed xml column, and using XQuery against a typed xml column. The three queries it uses are:

```
Dim sql_trad_getbank As String = "SELECT CustomerName, Demographics FROM Store"
Dim sql_xquery_getbank As String = "SELECT CustomerName, " _
    & "BankName =    Demographics.query('data(//BankName)') FROM Store"

Dim sql_xquery_getbank_typed As String = "SELECT    CustomerName, " &
    "BankName =    Demographics.query('declare    namespace
          x=""http://testschemas/StoreSurvey""; " _
    & "data(//x:BankName)') FROM StoreTyped"
```

The code to extract the rows records the current time, executes a command using the appropriate query, and then iterates through the rows adding the customer name and bank name to a StringBuilder. Once all the rows have been processed, the number of elapsed milliseconds is calculated, and this - together with the list of customer and bank names - is displayed in the page. This is the relevant section of code for the traditional (non-XQuery) approach:

```
Dim start As DateTime = DateTime.Now
con.Open()
reader = cmd.ExecuteReader(CommandBehavior.CloseConnection)
While reader.Read()
  Dim xd As New XmlDocument()
  xd.LoadXml(reader("Demographics"))
```

```vb
    Dim xn As XmlNode = xd.SelectSingleNode("//BankName")
    If Not xn Is Nothing Then
       builder.Append("Customer '" & reader("CustomerName") _
            & "' banks at " & xn.ChildNodes(0).Value & "<br />")
    End If
 End While
 Dim span As TimeSpan = DateTime.Now.Subtract(start)
 builder.Insert(0, String.Format("<p>Data access took {0} milliseconds</p>", _
            span.Milliseconds.ToString()))
 lblMessage.Text = builder.ToString()
```

The second and third options, executing an XQuery, use similar but much more compact code:

```vb
 Dim start As DateTime = DateTime.Now

 con.Open()
 reader = cmd.ExecuteReader(CommandBehavior.CloseConnection)
 While reader.Read()
   builder.Append("Customer '" & reader("CustomerName") _
            & "' banks at " & reader("BankName") & "<br />")
 End While
 Dim span As TimeSpan = DateTime.Now.Subtract(start)
 builder.Insert(0, String.Format("<p>Data access took {0} milliseconds</p>", _
            span.Milliseconds.ToString()))
 lblMessage.Text = builder.ToString()
```

Figure 2 shows the results of selecting the traditional approach, and you can see that - with the hardware we tested against - this took some 400 milliseconds to extract the data and process all the rows. This time includes that taken to manipulate the StringBuilder:

However, as you can see in Figure 3, data access times are considerably improved when using XQuery. For an un-typed xml column, the time taken to extract and process the same number of rows is some 25% less - the average on our system was around 300 milliseconds.

And even more striking is the performance when accessing a typed xml column. In this case the average access and processing time was around 220 milliseconds - a reduction against the traditional approach of some 45%. This is because SQL Server 2005 can shred the XML and store it in a more efficient manner, providing faster access when querying and when updating the content of XML documents.

And remember that this is with the database and Web server on the same machine, and includes the time for iterating the rows and building the display string in the StringBuilder.

The reduced network bandwidth usage when accessing a remote SQL Server will enhance the differences even more, but the percentage reduction in the actual data access times is impressive even when these factors aren't taken into account.

Parameters with XQuery

The next example, "*Using Parameters with an XQuery*", demonstrates some of the ways that you can pass parameter values to an XQuery, depending on how you want to specify the results that are included in the rowset returned by the query. As we discussed in the previous article, you can access the value of a T-SQL variable from within an XQuery or XPath statement using the sql:variable function.

The example provides four different queries that you can execute, including a stored procedure that executes an XQuery, and displays the results in an ASP.NET GridView control. Figure 4 shows the example page in action with the results of executing the stored procedure visible.

The first option selects rows using traditional T-SQL techniques, where the parameter is used in the WHERE clause. The value method of the Demographics column is used to extract the value of the NumberEmployees element, and cast it to an int data type so it can be compared directly to the value of the @emp parameter (of type SqlDbType.Int) that is passed to the query by a SqlParameter added to the command. The SELECT clause contains an XQuery that extracts just the value of the BankName element from the rows that match the expression in the WHERE clause. This produces the same result as you see in Figure 4:

```
SELECT CustomerName,

BankName = Demographics.query('data(//BankName)')
FROM Store
WHERE Demographics.value('(//NumberEmployees)[1]', 'int') > @emp
```

The second statement attempts to replace the WHERE clause with a condition within the XQuery itself. The call to the query method of the Demographics column includes an XPath that selects the value of the BankName element, but only where the StoreSurvey root element has a NumberEmployees element containing a value that matches the parameter passed to the statement.

Notice how the XPath number function is used to convert the data type of the NumberEmployees element with the data type of the parameter:

```
SELECT CustomerName,

BankName = Demographics.query('
        data(/StoreSurvey[number(NumberEmployees[1])        >
sql:variable("@emp")]/BankName)
')
FROM Store
```

However, this doesn't actually produce the result we want. If you run the example and select this option, you'll see that the rowset returned by the query contains **all** the rows from the table.

The bank name is NULL in rows where the number of employees is less than the value in the parameter passed to the query. This is a common mistake, and demonstrates how you have to be careful when using XQuery to select rows.

The third statement solves this problem by combining the XQuery selection technique with the use of a WHERE clause.

In this case, the exist method of the Demographics column is used to return either True or False, depending on whether there is a node in the XML document for this row that contains a NumberEmployees element with a value greater than the value of the @emp parameter (the syntax .[1] means "the first node of the current nodeset" - remember that the number function requires a single node, whereas the //NumberEmployees XPath statement returns a node collection even if there is only one node that matches).

And, again, the number function is used to ensure that the data types of the element value and the parameter value match:

```
SELECT CustomerName,

BankName = Demographics.query('data(//BankName)')
FROM Store
```

SQL Server Supporting Technology

```
WHERE    Demographics.exist('//NumberEmployees[number(.[1])   >
    sql:variable("@emp")]') = 1
```

The final option is a statement that just executes a stored procedure named GetBankNamesByEmployee within the database. The TSQL used in this stored procedure is the same as that described above (for the third option). However, it does demonstrate that you can use XQuery in just the same way in a stored procedure as you do in declarative and parameterized SQL statements:

```
CREATE PROCEDURE dbo.GetBankNamesByEmployee
@emp int AS
SELECT         CustomerName,        BankName      =
    Demographics.query('data(//BankName)')
FROM Store WHERE  Demographics.exist('//NumberEmployees[.    >
    sql:variable("@emp")]') = 1
```

Combining XQuery and XSL-T

Having seen how you can extract values from an XML document stored in SQL Server 2005, this next example changes direction somewhat by extracting an XML document of a specific format from the contents of an xml column, and then uses this XML to generate an HTML page by applying an XSL-T style sheet to the newly-generated XML. The SQL statement with its embedded XQuery looks like this:

```
SELECT Demographics.query('
  <sales-summary>
    <customer-name>{ sql:column("CustomerName") }</customer-name>
    <sales-data>
    <total-sales>{ data(//AnnualSales) }</total-sales>
    <employees>{ data(//NumberEmployees) }</employees>
    <sales-per-employee>
        {        round(number((//AnnualSales)[1])          div
number((//NumberEmployees)[1])) }
    </sales-per-employee>
    <store-size>{ data(//SquareFeet) }</store-size>
    <sales-per-sqssict>
     { round(number((//AnnualSales)[1]) div number((//SquareFeet)[1])) }
    </sales-per-sqssict>
   </sales-data>
  </sales-summary>
')
```

FROM Store WHERE CustomerID = @custid"

You can see that it creates an XML document with the root element sales-summary, and with two child elements. The first is a customer-name element, and this is followed by a sales-data element that itself contains five other items of sales-related information.

Notice how the sales-per-employee and sales-per-sqssict values can be calculated within the XQuery using the XPath number function and div operator. The result is then converted to a non-fractional number using the round function. The resulting XML document will look something like this:

```xml
<sales-summary>
  <customer-name>Acceptable Sales &amp; Service</customer-name>
  <sales-data>
    <total-sales>800000</total-sales>
    <employees>12</employees>
    <sales-per-employee>66667</sales-per-employee>
    <store-size>7000</store-size>
    <sales-per-sqssict>114</sales-per-sqssict>
  </sales-data>
</sales-summary>
```

The XSL-T Style Sheet

We then use a simple XSL-T style sheet to transform this XML into HTML. This is the style sheet:

```xml
<?xml version="1.0" encoding="UTF-8" ?>

<xsl:stylesheet version="1.0" xmlns:xsl="http://www.w3.org/1999/XSL/Transform">
  <xsl:template match="/">
    <html>
      <body>
        <b>
          Annual sales figures for customer
            '<xsl:apply-templates select="./sales-summary/customer-name" />'</b>
          <p />
          <xsl:apply-templates select="./sales-summary/sales-data" />
      </body>
```

```
        </html>
    </xsl:template>
    <xsl:template match="customer-name">
       <xsl:value-of select="."/>
    </xsl:template>
       <xsl:template match="total-sales">
      Your total annual sales are $<xsl:value-of select="."/><br />
    </xsl:template>
    <xsl:template match="employees">
      The number of people you employee is <xsl:value-of select="."/><br />
    </xsl:template>
    <xsl:template match="sales-per-employee">
        Your annual sales per employee are therefore $<xsl:value-of
select="."/><br />
    </xsl:template>
    <xsl:template match="store-size">
      Your store has a total square ssictage of <xsl:value-of select="."/><br />
    </xsl:template>
    <xsl:template match="sales-per-sqssict">
       This means that the annual sales per square ssict are $<xsl:value-of
select="."/><br />
    </xsl:template>
</xsl:stylesheet>
```

You can see that it creates the html and body elements, and - within the body element - applies a template that inserts the customer name into the output. Then it applies templates that match the five other elements within the nested sales-data element to insert these values and the appropriate accompanying text into the output.

Executing the XQuery

The relevant section of code in the ASP.NET page "*Combining XQuery and XSL-T*" that uses this XQuery and style sheet are shown next. The page uses an ASP.NET GridView control and a SqlDataSource control to display a list of customer names, as in the first two examples in this article.

Selecting a row in the GridView executes a routine named ShowSalesReport. This routine opens a connection to the database, creates a command, adds a parameter to specify the selected customer, and executes the SQL statement you saw earlier.

SQL Server Supporting Technology

The XML document returned from the query is accessed by calling the GetSqlXml method of the SqlDataReaderto get a SqlXml instance, which exposes the CreateReader method that we can use to get an XmlReader over the XML document itself. We do this, rather than extracting the value as a String, so that we can pass the reader to the Transform method of the XslCompiledTransform class later in our code:

```vb
Sub ShowSalesReport(ByVal sender As Object, ByVal e As EventArgs)
    Dim builder As New StringBuilder()
    Dim xmlr As XmlReader
    Using con As New SqlConnection(ConfigurationManager.ConnectionStrings _
                ("XMLTestConnectionString").ConnectionString)
        Dim cmd As New SqlCommand(sql_select, con)
        cmd.Parameters.Add(New SqlParameter("@custid", SqlDbType.Int))
                cmd.Parameters("@custid").Value = Int32.Parse(grid1.SelectedDataKey.Value)
        Try
          con.Open()
            Dim dr As SqlDataReader = cmd.ExecuteReader(CommandBehavior.CloseConnection)
          dr.Read()
          Dim oXML As SqlXml = dr.GetSqlXml(0)
          xmlr = CType(oXML.CreateReader(), XmlReader)
        Catch ex As Exception
          lblMessage.Text = ex.Message
          Return
        End Try
        ...
```

The next step is to create an instance of the XslCompiledTransform class, and load the XSL-T style sheet - this is stored in the data subfolder of the samples. Then we create a StreamWriter that will create the output file, and call the Transform method to generate the new HTML document. The second parameter to the Transform method is a reference to an XsltArgumentList instance, but as we have to arguments to pass to the style sheet we use Nothing for this parameter.

```vb
        ...
        Dim sPath As String = Path.Combine(Request.PhysicalApplicationPath, "data")
        Dim transform As New XslCompiledTransform()
        Try
```

SQL Server Supporting Technology

```
      transform.Load(Path.Combine(sPath, "sales-transform.xslt"))
        Using writer As New StreamWriter(Path.Combine(sPath, "sales-report.htm"))
          transform.Transform(xmlr, Nothing, writer)
        End Using
        lblMessage.Text = "Created sales report <a href='data/sales-report.htm' target='_blank'>" _
                & "sales-report.htm</a>"
      Catch ex As XsltException
        lblMessage.Text = ex.Message
      End Try
    End Using
  End Sub
```

The XslCompiledTransform class replaces the XslTransform class from earlier versions of the Framework. The XslCompiledTransform class compiles a style sheet into MSIL code, and so can achieve performance that is up to four times faster than the now deprecated XslTransform class.

Figure 5 shows this example page in action. You can see the hyperlink that is created after the new HTML file has been generated, and clicking on this hyperlink displays the HTML page in a new browser window.

We used a disk-based style sheet in this example, but that doesn't always have to the case. An XSL-T style sheet is, of course, a valid XML document in its own right. So you could just as easily store your style sheets in an xml column in a SQL Server 2005 database, and extract them as and when required.

Summary

In the previous article, we discussed the great new features in SQL Server 2005 that make it easier to work with XML documents, and also allows you to write more efficient data access code when you need to persist, access and update XML. SQL Server 2005 is not the first database to provide these features, but the combination of these new features and integration with ADO.NET make it easy to take advantage of them, while vastly reducing the amount of code you have to write.

In this article, you saw this demonstrated in several examples. We looked at some simple techniques for extracting data from an xml column using XQuery, and then compared the performance of XQuery with the traditional approach of loading the entire document into an XML parser and extracting the required values.

As you saw, XQuery reduces the bandwidth requirements by limiting the data returned over the network, removes the need to use an XML parser client-side, and dramatically reduces processing overhead and response times. And, when the XML document is stored in a typed xml column, the performance improvements are even more noticeable.

Then we looked at some different ways you can pass values to a query that contains an XQuery statement - pointing out one of the common pitfalls when selecting rows to be returned.

Finally, we saw how you can use XQuery to create custom XML documents from the data stored in an xml column, and then apply a style sheet to the result to transform it into any other format you might require. Of course, XQuery isn't limited to generating simple scalar values and XML documents or fragments.

You can use XQuery to generate any output you want, for example you could generate comma-separated or tab-separated data directly within your XQuery if this is the format that your applications require.

In the next and final article in this series, we'll delve deeper into XQuery and SQL Server 2005 XML features to see how we can improve performance when updating XML documents stored in the database, and how we can use XQuery within managed code stored procedures.

CHAPTER 11

Securing Information in 2005 and 2008 SQL Server

In this chapter, you will secure information.

You will:

- List the steps to be taken to protect information from unauthorized access.

- List the guidelines to be followed to prevent a virus attack.

SQL Server Supporting Technology

Introduction

Just as you have to take precautions for your own health and for the safety of your environment when using a computer, you must also take precautions to ensure the safety of the computer itself. In this chapter, you will familiarize yourself with the various threats to the information stored on your computer. You will also learn what steps you can take to ensure that these threats don't negatively affect your systems.

When you connect a computer to a network, you are making the information and the resources in it accessible to millions of unknown people with different motives. Not all are scrupulous. From a security perspective, this is a potential nightmare. You need to take proper steps to ensure the integrity of the information and resources in your computer.

Protect Information Security

You now see the importance of keeping your computer workspace safe and secure, and how doing so can benefit you and the people around you. Computer safety and security is not limited to the physical space around your computer; it also extends to the information contained within the computer itself.

In this chapter, you will identify methods of protecting your data. By connecting your computer to a network, you make the information and resources in it accessible to many other users. If someone with malicious intent accesses that information, they could potentially steal your personal files, your credit card information, or even your "virtual" identity. You need to take proper measures to secure the data in your computer to prevent others from misusing it.

Information Security

Information security is the process of protecting sensitive and essential information from unauthorized access, disclosure, destruction, or alteration. A *threat* is any circumstance or event with the potential to cause harm to an information system. A *security risk* is the possibility of a threat becoming a reality.

Hackers and Crackers

As with any society, ours has individuals whose intentions are less than good. Some individuals like to break into other people's computers as a hobby. Some do this for the challenge, much like a mountain climber looking to climb a mountain simply because it is there. In some cases, hackers claim that they don't intend to do any harm.

SQL Server Supporting Technology

They claim that they are performing a service by pointing out security leaks without performing any malicious acts to take advantage of those leaks. Hackers call those who break into systems with malicious intent crackers, and they make a distinction between the acts of hacking and cracking. The distinction, however, tends to be lost on those who are outside of the hacker community and who view any act of breaking into computer networks as criminal activity. Some individuals perform acts of vandalism, such as defacing websites by replacing the owner's content with their own content, often obscene or controversial.

User ID and Password

A *user ID* is the unique name provided to a computer user. This helps a computer network identify the user, every time the user logs in. User IDs are generally associated with a password. A *password* is a unique combination of characters that authenticates a user. Together, the user ID and password provide a user with access to information and resources on a computer network.

Access Rights

Access control is the assignment of *rights* and permissions for using local or network resources. It is important because it helps ensure the confidentiality, integrity, and availability of information and resources on a network. In larger networks, rights and permissions are granted by network administrative personnel, but in workgroups, a resource's owner is responsible for providing the proper level of access.

Protect Information Security

Implementing security measures prevents security risks from happening. The proactive steps to be followed to prevent security risks from happening include:

- Adopting an information security policy with respect to handling sensitive data. A security policy is the basic set of rules and guidelines that an organization will use to define its operations in regards to securing electronic data. At times, in some companies, the security policy will go beyond the electronic systems into paper data as well. To practice a security policy properly, the management of the company needs to be involved in the creation and execution of the directives that are outlined in the policy.

- Implementing procedures for reporting security incidents.

- Keeping staff members informed of a computer's weeknesses—of who has been accessing the resources, and how they have been gaining access. This information can help them identify where the servers and network are vulnerable, and deal with such vulnerabilities prudently. One good source of information is the security bulletins that are posted by software and hardware vendors. These bulletins identify security leaks that have been found in their products, and typically provide a work-around or a software upgrade to plug up the leak.

- Practicing good password policies. The primary purpose of a password is to ensure that no other user can log on using your name. A strong password that is not easily guessed by others protects the information stored on your computer. You should never share your passwords or keep them stored in a document on your computer. Someone could hack into your system and steal your passwords. You should also create passwords that would be difficult for someone to guess.

- Backing up the data and software on your computer to removable storage devices such as Zip disks or CD-ROMs. Network backups are typically run on a regularly scheduled timetable. It is strongly recommended that you perform regular backups of your own. Frequent and adequate backups protect against costly data losses, that could occur due to a computer malfunction or security breach.

Backing-Up Data

The aftermath of a computer crash or a security incident may be disastrous. It could destroy all the data on a hard drive, including all files and folders. Therefore, it is critical that you back up information in your computer to a removable storage device so that you have another kind of access to that information. Backing up data provides a cost-effective, easily manageable, and safer computing option.

Implications of Theft

You have to be aware of the fact that your information is vulnerable to theft. The implications of theft of a laptop, PDA, or mobile phone include:

- Possible misuse of confidential files.
- Loss of files.
- Loss of important contact details if not available on a separate source.
- Possible misuse of telephone numbers.

Preventing a Virus Attack

You have identified some of the ways in which you can protect your computer and the data contained within it. One of the most well-known ways in which data can be attacked, altered, or even destroyed is through viruses. In this topic, you will differentiate between different types of viruses, and adopt strategies to keep them out of your computer.

Just as humans can catch viruses that can lead to many different types of sicknesses and symptoms, computers can fall prey to the same "illnesses." You have likely heard news reports about the damage that can be caused by quickly and widely spreading computer viruses. In order to avoid becoming a victim of such an attack, you need to identify techniques to prevent—and, if necessary, contain and recover from—the adverse effects of a virus.

Computer Viruses

Viruses are small programs that attach themselves to files on the host computer. Viruses are typically spread when a file is copied from one computer to another. Because of the ease with which files are transferred across the Internet, the Internet has become a breeding ground for computer viruses. Some viruses do little more than replicate themselves. Others are designed to wreak havoc on the host computer, performing deeds such as erasing files or preventing important system functions from working properly. Viruses usually fall into one of three categories: boot-sector viruses, file infectors, and multipartite viruses.

Type	Description
Boot-sector viruses	Replace the code that normally resides in the master boot sector of a disk with their own viral code. They are spread by bootable floppy disks. When a system is booted with an infected disk, the virus loads into memory, and all subsequent disks used on that system will be infected by the virus. These viruses are no longer the primary source of infection. Symptoms of a boot-sector virus include receiving the message Missing Operating System or the message Hard Disk Not Found.
File infector viruses	Attach to executable files so that when the program is run, the virus is also run and loaded into memory.

	The virus then infects any other programs that are run on the system. There are two types of file infectors: macro viruses and worms. Macro viruses are encoded into a macro that's embedded into a document and are spread by sharing infected documents. The = main access point for macro viruses is as an email attachment. Symptoms include not being able to open or save files. Worm viruses are also becoming rampant. Worms are viruses that can replicate themselves and use memory, but don't attach themselves to other programs.
Multipartite viruses	Have the characteristics of both boot-sector viruses and file infector viruses.

Antivirus Software

Antivirus software is a program that is used to detect and remove a virus. Removing a virus is also known as disinfecting. Antivirus software usually includes two components: a scanner that detects viruses before they can infect the computer, and a repair program that deletes viruses that have successfully infected the computer. If a virus has infected your computer, you can:

- Repair or delete the infected file, if it is a known piece of malicious code.

- Quarantine the infected file, if it is a piece of malicious code that you suspect is not yet known, so that it cannot be opened or executed.

Limitations of Antivirus

New viruses are released every day, but antivirus software is programmed to trap only known viruses. Vendors of antivirus software typically release periodic updates that allow them to deal with new viruses that have been discovered since the last release. One limitation of using antivirus software is that you have to keep updating it to prevent data loss.

The second limitation is that even though you keep updating your antivirus, there are times when new viruses strike long before software vendors are aware of it.

SQL Server Supporting Technology

Preventing a Virus Attack

Virus infection can be very expensive in terms of time, data loss, and money. The best way to deal with viruses is to put measures into place that avoid infection. To prevent a virus attack on your machine, you need to practice the following steps:

- Do not open any files attached to an email unless you know what it is, even if it appears to come from a friend, or someone you know. Some viruses can replicate themselves and spread through email. Better be safe than sorry and confirm that the person you know really sent it.

- Do not open any files attached to an email if the subject line is questionable or unexpected.

- If there is a need to open it, always save the file to your hard drive before opening it.

- Delete chain and junk emails. Do not forward or reply to them. These types of email are considered spam, which is unsolicited, intrusive mail that clogs up the network.
- Do not download any files from strangers.

- Exercise caution when downloading files from the Internet. Ensure that the source is a legitimate and reputable one.

- Verify that an antivirus program checks the files on the download site. If you are uncertain, do not download the file at all or download the file to a floppy disk and test it with antivirus software.

- Do not share floppy disks between computers.

- Do not boot a computer with a startup disk that has been used in another computer.

- Write protect all boot diskettes.

Threat and Vulnerability Mitigation (Database Engine 2008)

Although SQL Server includes a variety of security mechanisms, every system has features that could be exploited for malicious purposes. This page provides links to

SQL Server Supporting Technology

help you locate the information that you need about threats and vulnerabilities in the SQL Server Database Engine, and how you can eliminate them.

CHAPTER 12

SQL Server 2008 New Features

In this chapter you will learn:

- Security and Data Auditing
- Availability and Reliability
- SQL Server Management
- Feature Deprecation

SQL Server Supporting Technology

Introduction

Let's jump into each the of new SQL Server 2008 product categories, features and provide references to some of these technologies as additional points of reference.

Security and Data Auditing

- Transparent Data Encryption - This is encrypting the data while it is on disk and remains transparent to applications

- External Key Management - This new functionality relates to consolidation of key management and integration with external products

- Data Auditing - This is one core feature of SQL Server 2008 that will include a number of new features to include:

  - The introduction of first class 'AUDIT' objects
  - Auditing DDL (data definition language) commands
  - Support for multiple logging targets

Availability and Reliability

- CPUs - Support for pluggable CPUs which means that a CPU can be added on the fly and recognized by SQL Server 2008 just like memory in SQL Server 2005

- Database Mirroring - Enhanced Database Mirroring to include compression of mirror streams, enhanced performance and automatic page-level repair for the principal and mirror.

Performance

- Data Compression - This new feature provides the ability to easily enable or disable data compression as an online command as well as offer more efficient data storage above and beyond traditional data compression

SQL Server Supporting Technology

- Backup Stream Compression - The ability to configure compression with server level control or backup statement control of all backup types (full, differential, transaction log)

- Performance Data Collection - When you are experiencing a performance issue the biggest problem is pinpointing the problem, so with SQL Server 2008 Microsoft is introducing a single common framework for performance related data collection, reporting, and warehousing

- Improved Plan Guide Support - With SQL Server 2008 plans can be frozen for permanent query usage as well as pull plans directly from plan cache with SQL Server Management Studio integration

- Resource Governor - If you have had the need to segment your SQL Server resource utilization then you should be looking forward to SQL Server 2008 because you will have the opportunity to create pools and groups to segment the resources and govern them independently

Management

- Policy-Based Management Framework - The ability to manage objects via policies as opposed to traditional scripts with inherent monitoring and enforcement

- Microsoft System Center - Integration with Microsoft System Center which a product from Microsoft to improve operational costs

- Extended Events - Another new feature is Extended Events which is a high performance yet light weight tracing infrastructure with insight into the core engine independent of SQL Trace

New Data Types

- Date Time Data Type - The datetime data type will now be able to support the following:

  - Precision to the 100th nanosecond which is 7 digits past second.

  - Time-zone datetime offset to translate the datetimes across numerous time zones.

  - Rather than having to parse the datatime for just the date or just the time, now SQL Server 2008 will have date only support as well as time only support

SQL Server Supporting Technology

- HierarchyID - With the introduction of the HierarchyID data type this data type will be hierarchical-aware and will be accompanied by built-in functions, methods, etc. to support complex hierarchies in your data with .NET

Development Enhancements

- Entity Data Model - With SQL Server 2008 will come the concept of a 'business entities' vs. tables, this will enable the ability to model more complex relationships as well as be able to retrieve entities as opposed to a result set of rows and columns

- LINQ- LINQ is a new .NET Framework that encompass language-integrated query, set, and transform operations

- SQL Server Change Tracking - This feature provides the ability to have change data capture without a comparable value

- Table Valued Parameters - Ability to create variables of a table value data type and be able to pass this variable into a stored procedure

- MERGE statement - Another term for this new feature is 'upsert'; this commands provides the ability to programmatically INSERT data if it does not exist or UPDATE the data if it does all in 1 set of logic.

- Large UDT's - The 8000 byte limit is no longer applicable for on CLR-based UDTs and UDAs

- Spatial data - SQL Server 2008 will support GEOMETRY and GEOGRAPHY data types with built-in spatial function support and spatial indexes to support more GIS needs.

- XML enhancements (support for lax validation, office 12 support, xs:dateTime support, lists/union types, LET FLOWR support, etc.)

Service Broker

Interface - A new user interface and tools will be released for working with Service Broker in order to add, drop or edit Service Broker objects directly in SQL Server Management Studio .

SQL Server Supporting Technology

Conversation Priority

The ability to set message ordering with a send and receive impact with levels one to ten:

- Data Storage

- Data Compression - Reference the Performance section above.

- FILESTREAM Attribute - With this feature get the best of both worlds with functionality from BLOBs in the DB vs. BLOBs on filesystem

- Integrated Full Text Search - With SQL Server 2008 Full Text Search is fully integrated into the relational engine with no external storage, no external service as well as more efficient and reliable costing.

- Sparse columns - SQL Server 2008 has more efficient storage for 'wide' tables with many columns that repeat and do not contain data

- New index types - New indexes include:
  - Spatial indexes
  - Hierarchical indexes
  - FILTERED indexes (indexes on filtered values within columns)

Data Warehousing/ETL

- Partitioned Table Parallelism - This feature eliminates the one thread limit per partition.

- Star Join support - SQL Server 2008 now supports a star join with no special syntax which is completely optimizer based with full backward syntax support.

  - Data compression - Reference the Performance section above

  - Resource Governor - Reference the Performance section above.

  - Persistent Lookups in SSIS - There is no longer a need for re-querying for lookup operators and cache lookups in multiple ways with the ability to persist lookups to disk.

SQL Server Supporting Technology

- Improved thread scheduling in SSIS - This is accomplished by a shared thread pool and pipeline parallelism

- SQL Server Change Tracking - Reference the Development Enhancements section above.

- MERGE statement - The MERGE statement will add a great deal of value with slowly changing dimensions.

- Scale-out analysis services - With read-only storage multiple Analysis Services SQL Servers can be leveraged

- Subspace computations

- New tools for cube design

- Best practice design alerting

- Backup cubes with better scalability

- Excel - Data-mining add-ins for Excel

Reporting

- Reporting Services Deployment - IIS is no longer required to run Reporting Services
- Rich-text support
- Enhanced visualization graphing
- Word - Reports can be rendered to Microsoft Word

Deprecation

- Many of the 'old' features are removed to include:
  - 60, 65 and/or 70 compatibility modes
  - NOLOG and/or TRUNCATEONLY for the BACKUP command

CHAPTER 13

SQL Server 2008 Planning and Architecture

In this chapter you will learn about:

- Logs logical and Physical Architecture
- Transactional Logs Write-backs

SQL Server Supporting Technology

Log Logical Architecture

Engine is the core service for storing, processing, and securing data. The Database Engine provides controlled access and rapid transaction processing to meet the requirements of the most demanding data consuming applications within your enterprise.

Use the Database Engine to create relational databases for online transaction processing or online analytical processing data. This includes creating tables for storing data, and database objects such as indexes, views, and stored procedures for viewing, managing, and securing data. You can use SQL Server Management Studio to manage the database objects, and SQL Server Profiler for capturing server events.

The SQL Server transaction log operates logically as if the transaction log is a string of log records. Each log record is identified by a log sequence number (LSN). Each new log record is written to the logical end of the log with an LSN that is higher than the LSN of the record before it.

Log records are stored in a serial sequence as they are created. Each log record contains the ID of the transaction that it belongs to. For each transaction, all log records associated with the transaction are individually linked in a chain using backward pointers that speed the rollback of the transaction.

Log records for data modifications record either the logical operation performed or they record the before and after images of the modified data. The before image is a copy of the data before the operation is performed; the after image is a copy of the data after the operation has been performed.

Logical operation logged

- To roll the logical operation forward, the operation is performed again.
- To roll the logical operation back, the reverse logical operation is performed.
- Before and after image logged
- To roll the operation forward, the after image is applied.
- To roll the operation back, the before image is applied.
- Many types of operations are recorded in the transaction log. These operations include:

SQL Server Supporting Technology

- The start and end of each transaction.

- Every data modification (insert, update, or delete). This includes changes by system stored procedures or data definition language (DDL) statements to any table, including system tables.

- Every extent and page allocation or deallocation.

- Creating or dropping a table or index.

- Rollback operations are also logged. Each transaction reserves space on the transaction log to make sure that enough log space exists to support a rollback that is caused by either an explicit rollback statement or if an error is encountered. The amount of space reserved depends on the operations performed in the transaction, but generally is equal to the amount of space used to log each operation. This reserved space is freed when the transaction is completed.

- The section of the log file from the first log record that must be present for a successful database-wide rollback to the last-written log record is called the active part of the log, or the *active log*. This is the section of the log required to do a full recovery of the database. No part of the active log can ever be truncated.

Log Physical Architecture

The transaction log is used to guarantee the data integrity of the database and for data recovery. The topics in this section provide the information about the physical architecture of the transaction log. Understanding the physical architecture can improve your effectiveness in managing transaction logs.

The transaction log in a database maps over one or more physical files. Conceptually, the log file is a string of log records. Physically, the sequence of log records is stored efficiently in the set of physical files that implement the transaction log.

The SQL Server Database Engine divides each physical log file internally into a number of virtual log files. Virtual log files have no fixed size, and there is no fixed number of virtual log files for a physical log file. The Database Engine chooses the size of the virtual log files dynamically while it is creating or extending log files. The Database Engine tries to maintain a small number of virtual files. The size of the virtual files after a log file has been extended is the sum of the size of the existing log and the size of the new file increment. The size or number of virtual log files cannot be configured or set by administrators.

The only time virtual log files affect system performance is if the log files are defined by small *size* and *growth_increment* values. If these log files grow to a large size because of many small increments, they will have lots of virtual log files. This can slow down database startup and also log backup and restore operations. We recommend that you assign log files a *size* value close to the final size required, and also have a relatively large *growth_increment* value

The transaction log is a wrap-around file. For example, consider a database with one physical log file divided into four virtual log files. When the database is created, the logical log file begins at the start of the physical log file.

New log records are added at the end of the logical log and expand toward the end of the physical log. Log truncation frees any virtual logs whose records all appear in front of the minimum recovery log sequence number (MinLSN). The *MinLSN* is the log sequence number of the oldest log record that is required for a successful database-wide rollback. The transaction log in the example database would look similar to the one in the following illustration.

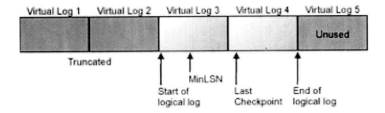

When the end of the logical log reaches the end of the physical log file, the new log records wrap around to the start of the physical log file.

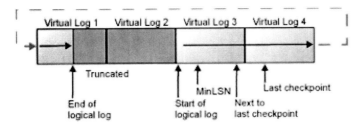

This cycle repeats endlessly, as long as the end of the logical log never reaches the beginning of the logical log. If the old log records are truncated frequently enough to always leave sufficient room for all the new log records created through the next checkpoint, the log never fills. However, if the end of the logical log does reach the start of the logical log, one of two things occurs:

If the FILEGROWTH setting is enabled for the log and space is available on the disk, the file is extended by the amount specified in *growth_increment* and the new log records are added to the extension.

If the FILEGROWTH setting is not enabled, or the disk that is holding the log file has less free space than the amount specified in *growth_increment*, an 9002 error is generated.

If the log contains multiple physical log files, the logical log will move through all the physical log files before it wraps back to the start of the first physical log file.

Write-Ahead Transaction Log

[This topic is pre-release documentation and is subject to change in future releases. Blank topics are included as placeholders.]

This topic describes the role of the write-ahead transaction log in recording data modifications to disk. For basic information about transaction logs, see Introduction to Transaction Logs.

SQL Server uses a write-ahead log (WAL), which guarantees that no data modifications are written to disk before the associated log record is written to disk. This maintains the ACID properties for a transaction. For more information about transactions and ACID properties, see Transactions (Database Engine).

To understand how the write-ahead log works, it is important for you to know how modified data is written to disk. SQL Server maintains a buffer cache into which it reads data pages when data must be retrieved. Data modifications are not made directly to disk, but are made to the copy of the page in the buffer cache. The modification is not written to disk until a checkpoint occurs in the database, or the modification must be written to disk so the buffer can be used to hold a new page. Writing a modified data page from the buffer cache to disk is called flushing the page. A page modified in the cache, but not yet written to disk, is called a *dirty page*.

SQL Server Supporting Technology

At the time a modification is made to a page in the buffer, a log record is built in the log cache that records the modification. This log record must be written to disk before the associated dirty page is flushed from the buffer cache to disk. If the dirty page is flushed before the log record is written, the dirty page creates a modification on the disk that cannot be rolled back if the server fails before the log record is written to disk. SQL Server has logic that prevents a dirty page from being flushed before the associated log record is written. Log records are written to disk when the transactions are committed.

INDEX

A

Access Rights · 159
aggregation · 102
Ancestor · 31
Ancestors · 31, 128
Ancestry · 31
Antivirus Software · 162
APIs · 69, 70, 76
Application integration · 58
Applications · 144
Atomic values · 127
attribute · 18, 27, 28, 35, 36, 37, 38, 41, 42, 43, 50, 51, 52, 53, 54, 56, 58, 61, 62, 64, 77, 82, 83, 86, 87, 95, 97, 98, 106, 108, 113, 114, 119, 126, 127, 131, 132, 134, 135
Attribute · 37, 38, 43, 50, 56, 75, 83, 97
Axes · 133

B

Broken XML Files · 49

C

CDATA · 42, 50, 77
Child · 29
Children · 127
Comment · 41, 121
Comparisons · 105
conditional expressions · 103
Conditional Expressions · 104
context item · 103, 112
context position · 103
context size · 103

Crackers · 158
Creates · 107

D

Data exchange · 58
datatype expressions · 103
date and time · 103, 110, 125
Declaration · 39, 43, 46, 50, 51, 58, 84
default prefix · 110
default-namespace · 63
Defining Elements · 59
Descendant · 32
Descendants · 30, 128
DOCTYPE · 46, 47, 49
Document Structure · 58
Document Type Definition · 39, 45, 46, 49
DOM · 35, 69, 70, 75, 76, 77, 106
DTD · 39, 45, 46, 47, 49, 50, 51, 52, 53, 54, 55, 77

E

element · 17, 18, 27, 28, 29, 30, 31, 32, 33, 34, 35, 36, 37, 38, 40, 42, 43, 44, 46, 48, 49, 50, 52, 53, 54, 55, 56, 58, 59, 60, 61, 62, 63, 64, 65, 66, 67, 75, 78, 80, 82, 83, 86, 88, 89, 95, 96, 97, 98, 102, 104, 105, 106, 107, 108, 109, 110, 112, 113, 118, 119, 121, 124, 125, 126, 127, 128, 129, 130, 131, 132, 133, 134, 138, 140, 146, 149, 150, 152, 153
Element · 17, 28, 29, 31, 32, 34, 37, 48, 50, 55, 59, 76, 82, 95, 106, 126, 127
Element Type Declaration · 50
element_name · 17
Empty Elements · 17
entities · 27, 38, 39, 40, 46, 48, 50, 51, 52
Entities · 38, 48, 51, 52
Entity · 38, 39, 40, 48, 51, 76
Expression Language · 101, 103
extensible · 20, 53, 55

F

FLWOR · 103, 115, 117
FLWR expressions · 109
functions · 60, 103, 106, 108, 110, 111, 119, 125, 126, 139, 161

G

General Guidelines · 118

H

Hackers · 158, 159
HTML · 16, 17, 18, 19, 20, 22, 25, 39, 41, 82, 92, 93, 94, 97, 100, 107, 113, 114, 124, 151, 152, 154, 155
hypertext · 17, 18
HyperText Markup Language · 16

I

Information Security · 158, 159
Insert XML Entities · 40
Introduction · 16, 27, 28, 46, 58, 70, 91, 99, 123, 127, 128, 129, 133, 137, 142, 158
Items · 127

L

Location Path Expression · 134
Lorel · 102
Lower · 17

M

Method · 72
Microsoft technology · 82
Mixed processing · 122

N

Namespace · 42, 43, 61, 62, 63, 65, 66, 83, 84, 85, 86, 87, 88, 96
namespaces · 27, 42, 43, 44, 53, 58, 60, 61, 62, 63, 64, 65, 67, 82, 83, 84, 86, 87, 88, 103, 105
Namespaces · 42, 43, 60, 61, 63, 65, 67, 82, 83, 84, 85, 86, 87, 88, 100, 124
Native XML processing is · 119
Node Values and Expressions · 106
Non-default namespaces · 66

O

Object · 70, 145, 154
Output · 94

P

parameter entity · 52
Parent · 29
platform independent · 16, 20
Predicates · 130, 131
Primitive Data Types · 106
Processing Instruction · 40, 41
Proper Nesting · 48

Q

QName manipulation · 110, 125
quantified expressions · 103
Quilt · 102

R

Recognizing Conflict · 81
Relational XML processing · 119
Relationship of Nodes · 127
Relative Location · 129
role of namespaces · 63
Root · 28, 48, 95

S

SAX · 35, 69, 76, 77, 78, 79, 80
schema · 45, 47, 53, 54, 55, 56, 60, 122, 143
Schema · 53, 54, 55, 61, 83, 124
Schema of Schemas · 54
Select all book Nodes · 138
Select the First book Node · 138
Selecting and Filtering Elements · 115
Selecting Nodes · 129, 137
Selecting Several Paths · 132

Selecting Unknown Nodes · 132
Self Evaluation · 105
Sequences · 107, 109
SGML · 18, 20, 22, 23, 24, 25
Shredding with coarse XML fragments · 122
Shredding with fine XML fragments · 122Sibling · 33
Siblings · 33, 127
Sorting and Context · 112
start tag · 18, 36, 38, 44, 55, 60, 134
Storing XML in a Database · 142, 143
Storing XML in a Database 2005 · 143
Stylesheet Reference · 96
SUMMARY · 67, 89
syntax · 21, 27, 37, 39, 41, 49, 50, 51, 53, 55, 59, 84, 95, 101, 102, 104, 105, 108, 125, 135, 150
Syntax Overview · 96

T

Technical Architecture · 67
template Match · 97
The for Clause · 115
The let Clause · 116
The order by Clause · 117
The return Clause · 117
The Tree Structure · 29
The where Clause · 117
Things not covered here · 119
Tree Rules · 30
Type Specification · 112

U

Universal Resource Identifier · 42
Upper · 17
URI · 42, 43, 44, 49, 52, 55, 60, 62, 64, 65, 66, 67, 83, 84, 95
User ID and Password · 159

V

Valid XML · 49
validation · 41, 46, 47, 54, 61, 92, 143
variables · 51, 103, 105, 107

Vertical Bar · 139

W

W3C · 18, 35, 43, 45, 53, 55, 61, 62, 67, 83, 84, 85, 87, 92, 101, 124, 125, 131, 138, 143
Web applications · 58
well-formed · 27, 28, 34, 35, 36, 38, 39, 40, 42, 44, 46, 47, 48, 49, 53, 55, 57, 58, 63, 95, 98
Well-formed · 34, 47
Well-Formed · 48
What You Should Already Know · 100, 124
Whitespace · 35
Workaround · 138
World Wide Web · 18

X

XHTML · 43, 82, 83, 100, 122, 124
XML · 18, 19, 20, 22, 23, 58, 59, 61, 63, 64, 65
XML Code · 93
XML Data · 100, 141
XML databases · 109, 119, 122
XML Declaration · 35, 95
XML Document · 40, 45, 76
XML documents · 19, 21, 23, 34, 40, 42, 45, 46, 49, 53, 62, 63, 69, 70, 76, 77, 92, 101, 119, 124, 125, 126, 142, 143, 149, 155, 156
XML elements · 27, 31, 48, 58, 60, 62, 132
XML namespace · 43, 44, 61, 62, 63, 83
XML Parser · 35
XML Schema · 53, 61, 63, 82, 102, 106, 111, 112
XML Shredding · 119
XML Tag · 28
xmlns · 42, 43, 44, 62, 63, 65, 66, 82, 83, 84, 85, 86, 87, 88, 93, 95, 98, 152
XML-QL · 102
xml-stylesheet · 41, 93, 94, 96, 97
XPath · 35, 92, 93, 98, 100, 102, 103, 104, 108, 119, 123, 124, 125, 126, 129, 132, 133, 134, 136, 138, 139, 140, 146, 149, 150, 152
XQuery · 99, 100, 101, 102, 103, 104, 105, 106, 107, 108, 109, 110, 111, 112, 113, 114, 115, 116, 117, 119, 121, 122, 124, 125, 126, 139, 141, 142, 143, 144, 146, 147, 148, 149, 150, 151, 152, 153, 155, 156
xsl · 93, 94, 95, 96, 97, 98, 106, 152, 153
XSLT · 22, 35, 62, 91, 92, 93, 94, 95, 96, 97, 98, 109, 124, 125, 126, 139

SQL Server Supporting Technology

Y

YATL · 102

Behavior Changes to Database Engine Features in SQL Server 2008

This topic describes the changes in behavior of some Database Engine features in SQL Server 2008 from their behavior in earlier versions of SQL Server.

Query Processor Architecture

SQL Server 2008 changes the way queries on partitioned tables and indexes are processed. Queries on partitioned objects that use the USE PLAN hint for a plan generated by SQL Server 2005 might contain an invalid plan. For more information, see Considerations for Upgrading the Database Engine. For more information about query processing on partitioned objects, see Query Processing Enhancements on Partitioned Tables and Indexes.

Linked Servers

SQL Server 2008 changes the transaction semantics of INSERT...EXECUTE statements that execute against a loopback linked server. In SQL Server 2005, this scenario is not supported and causes an error. In SQL Server 2008, an INSERT...EXECUTE statement can execute against a loopback linked server when the connection does not have multiple active result sets (MARS) enabled. When MARS is enabled on the connection, the behavior is the same as in SQL Server 2005.

Breaking Changes to Database Engine Features in SQL Server 2008

This topic describes the changes made to the Database Engine in SQL Server 2008 that could cause applications that are based on earlier versions of SQL Server to break.

Common Language Runtime (CLR)

Feature	Description
CLR Assemblies	When a database is upgraded to SQL Server 2008, the **Microsoft.SqlServer.Types** assembly to support the **hierarchyid** data type is automatically be installed. Upgrade advisor rules detect any user type or assemblies with conflicting names. The upgrade advisor will advise renaming of any conflicting assembly, and either renaming any conflicting type, or using two-part names in the code to refer to that preexisting user type. If a database upgrade detects a user assembly with conflicting name, it will automatically rename that assembly and put the database into suspect mode. If a user type with conflicting name exists during the upgrade, no special steps are taken. After the upgrade, both the old user type, and the new system type, will exist. The user type will be available only through two-part names.

DBCC

Feature	Description
Logical consistency checking on indexes by DBCC CHECKDB or DBCC CHECKTABLE	Logical consistency checking on indexes varies according to the compatibility level of the database, as follows: • If the compatibility level is 100 (SQL Server 2008) or higher: • Unless NOINDEX is specified, DBCC CHECKDB or DBCC CHECKTABLE performs both physical and logical consistency checks on a single table and on all its nonclustered indexes. However, on XML indexes, spatial indexes, and indexed views only physical consistency checks are performed by default.

- If WITH EXTENDED_LOGICAL_CHECKS is specified, logical checks are performed on an indexed view, XML indexes, and spatial indexes, where present. By default, physical consistency checks are performed before the logical consistency checks. If NOINDEX is also specified, only the logical checks are performed. These logical consistency checks cross check the internal index table of the index object with the user table that it is referencing. To find outlying rows, an internal query is constructed to perform a full intersection of the internal and user tables. Running this query can have a very high effect on performance, and its progress cannot be tracked. Therefore, we recommend that you specify WITH EXTENDED_LOGICAL_CHECKS only if you suspect index issues that are unrelated to physical corruption, or if page-level checksums have been turned off and you suspect column-level hardware corruption.
- If the compatibility level is 90 or less, unless NOINDEX is specified, DBCC CHECKDB or DBCC CHECKTABLE performs both physical and logical consistency checks on a single table or indexed view and on all its nonclustered and XML indexes. Spatial indexes are not supported.

Dynamic Management Views

View	Description
sys.dm_os_sys_info	• Removed the **cpu_ticks_in_ms** and **sqlserver_start_time_cpu_ticks** columns.

Transact-SQL

Feature	Description
CONVERT	If an invalid style is passed to the CONVERT function, an error is returned when the type of conversion is binary to character or character to binary. In earlier versions of SQL Server, the invalid style was set to the default style for binary-to-character and character-to-binary conversions.

Discontinued Database Engine Functionality in SQL Server 2008

The following table shows Database Engine features from earlier versions of SQL Server that are not supported in SQL Server 2008.

Category	Discontinued feature	Replacement
Aliases	sp_addalias	Replace aliases with a combination of user accounts and database roles. For more information, see CREATE USER (Transact-SQL) and CREATE ROLE (Transact-SQL). Remove aliases in upgraded databases by using sp_dropalias.
APIs	Registered Servers API	Replaced by a new registered servers API that supports new SQL Server 2008 features.
Backup and restore	DUMP statement	BACKUP
Backup and restore	LOAD statement	RESTORE
Backup and restore	BACKUP LOG WITH NO_LOG	None. The transaction log is automatically truncated when the database is using the simple recovery model. If you must remove the log backup chain from a database, switch to the simple recovery model.
Backup and restore	BACKUP LOG WITH TRUNCATE_ONLY	None. The transaction log is automatically truncated when the database is using the simple recovery model. If you must remove the log backup chain from a database, switch to the simple recovery model.
Backup and restore	BACKUP TRANSACTION	BACKUP LOG
Backup and restore	sp_helpdevice	Query the **sys.backup_devices** catalog view.
Compatibility	60, 65, and 70	Databases must be set to at least compatibility level

SQL Server Supporting Technology

level	compatibility levels	80.
DBCC	DBCC CONCURRENCYVIOLATION	None
Groups	**sp_addgroup**	Use roles.
Groups	**sp_changegroup**	Use roles.
Groups	**sp_dropgroup**	Use roles.
Groups	**sp_helpgroup**	Use roles.
Sample databases	**Northwind** and **pubs**	Use **AdventureWorks**. **Northwind** and **pubs** are available as downloads, or can be copied from a previous installation of SQL Server. For more information, see AdventureWorks Sample Databases.
Tools	Surface Area Configuration Tool	The Surface Area Configuration Tool is discontinued for SQL Server 2008. For more information, see Backward Compatibility.

Deprecated Database Engine Features in SQL Server 2008

Introduction

Deprecated features include features that will not be supported in the next version of SQL Server and features that will not be supported in a future version of SQL Server. The usage of deprecated features can be monitored by using the SQLServer:Deprecated Features object performance counter and trace events. For more information about how to monitor events, see Using SQL Server Objects.

Features Not Supported in the Next Version of SQL Server

The following SQL Server Database Engine features will not be supported in the next version of SQL Server. Do not use these features in new development work, and modify applications that currently use these features as soon as possible. The **Feature name** column appears in trace events as the ObjectName, in performance counters and **sys.dm_os_performance_counters** as the instance_name. The Feature ID appears in trace events as the ObjectId.

Category	Deprecated feature	Replacement	Feature name
Backup and restore	BACKUP { DATABASE | LOG } WITH PASSWORD	None	BACKUP DATABASE or LOG WITH PASSWORD
Backup and restore	BACKUP { DATABASE | LOG } WITH MEDIAPASSWORD	None	BACKUP DATABASE or LOG WITH MEDIAPASSWORD
Backup and Restore	RESTORE { DATABASE | LOG } ... WITH DBO_ONLY	RESTORE { DATABASE | LOG } ... ... WITH RESTRICTED_USER	RESTORE DATABASE or LOG WITH DBO_ONLY
Backup and restore	RESTORE { DATABASE | LOG } WITH PASSWORD	None	RESTORE DATABASE or LOG WITH PASSWORD
Backup and restore	RESTORE { DATABASE | LOG } WITH MEDIAPASSWORD	None	RESTORE DATABASE or LOG WITH MEDIAPASSWORD

SQL Server Supporting Technology

Compatibility levels	80 compatibility level and upgrade from version 80.	Compatibility levels are only available for the last two versions. For more information about compatibility levels, see ALTER DATABASE Compatibility Level (Transact-SQL).	Database compatibility level 80
Metadata	DATABASEPROPERTY	DATABASEPROPERTYEX	DATABASEPROPERTY
Database objects	WITH APPEND clause on triggers	Re-create the whole trigger.	CREATE TRIGGER WITH APPEND
Instance options	Default setting of **disallow results from triggers** option = 0	Default setting of **disallow results from triggers** option = 1	sp_configure 'disallow results from triggers'
Database options	sp_dboption	ALTER DATABASE	sp_dboption
Query hints	FASTFIRSTROW hint	OPTION (FAST n).	FASTFIRSTROW
Remote servers	sp_addremotelogin	Replace remote servers by using linked servers.	sp_addremotelogin
	sp_addserver		sp_addserver
	sp_dropremotelogin		sp_dropremotelogin
	sp_helpremotelogin		sp_helpremotelogin
	sp_remoteoption		sp_remoteoption
Remote servers	@@remserver	Replace remote servers by using linked servers.	None
Remote servers	SET REMOTE_PROC_TRANSACTIONS	Replace remote servers by using linked servers.	SET REMOTE_PROC_TRANSACTIONS
Security	sp_dropalias	Replace aliases with a combination of user accounts and database roles. Use **sp_dropalias** to remove aliases in upgraded databases.	sp_dropalias
SET options	SET DISABLE_DEF_CNST_CHK	None. Option has no	SET DISABLE_DEF_CNST_CHK

SQL Server Supporting Technology

		effect.	
SET options	SET ROWCOUNT for INSERT, UPDATE, and DELETE statements	TOP keyword	SET ROWCOUNT
Transact-SQL syntax	Use of *= and =*	Use ANSI join syntax. For more information, see FROM (Transact-SQL).	Non-ANSI *= or =* outer join operators
Transact-SQL syntax	COMPUTE / COMPUTE BY	Use ROLLUP	COMPUTE [BY]
System tables	**sys.database_principal_aliases**	Use roles instead of aliases.	**database_principal_aliases**
Transact-SQL	The RAISERROR (Format: RAISERROR integer string) syntax is deprecated.	Rewrite the statement using the current RAISERROR syntax.	Oldstyle RAISEERROR
Other	DB-Library Embedded SQL for C	Although the Database Engine still supports connections from existing applications that use the DB-Library and Embedded SQL APIs, it does not include the files or documentation required to do programming work on applications that use these APIs. A future version of the SQL Server Database Engine will drop support for connections from DB-Library or Embedded SQL applications. Do not use DB-Library or Embedded SQL to develop new applications. Remove any dependencies on either DB-Library or Embedded SQL when you are modifying existing applications. Instead of these APIs, use the **SQLClient**	None

SQL Server Supporting Technology

	namespace or an API such as OLE DB or ODBC. SQL Server 2008 does not include the DB-Library DLL required to run these applications. To run DB-Library or Embedded SQL applications, you must have available the DB-Library DLL from SQL Server version 6.5, SQL Server 7.0, or SQL Server 2000.

Features Not Supported in a Future Version of SQL Server

The following SQL Server Database Engine features are supported in the next version of SQL Server, but will be removed in a later version. The specific version of SQL Server has not been determined.

Category	Deprecated feature	Replacement	Feature name
Compatibility levels	sp_dbcmptlevel	ALTER DATABASE … SET COMPATIBILITY_LEVEL. For more information, see ALTER DATABASE Compatibility Level (Transact-SQL).	sp_dbcmptlevel
Compatibility levels	Database compatibility level 90	Plan to upgrade the database and application for a future release.	Database compatibility level 90
XML	Inline XDR Schema Generation	The XMLDATA directive to the FOR XML option is deprecated. Use XSD generation in the case of RAW and AUTO	XMLDATA

SQL Server Supporting Technology

		modes. There is no replacement for the XMLDATA directive in EXPLICT mode.	
Backup and restore	sp_helpdevice	sys.backup_devices	sp_helpdevice
Collations	Korean_Wansung_Unicode Lithuanian_Classic SQL_AltDiction_CP1253_CS_AS	None. These collations exist in SQL Server 2005, but are not visible through **fn_helpcollations**.	Korean_Wansung_Unicode Lithuanian_Classic SQL_AltDiction_CP1253_CS_AS
Collations	Hindi Macedonian	These collations exist in SQL Server 2005, but are not visible through **fn_helpcollations**. Use Macedonian_FYROM_90 and Indic_General_90 instead.	Hindi Macedonian
Connections	SQLOLEDB is not a supported provider.	Use SQL Server Native Client for ad hoc connections.	OLEDB for ad hoc connections
Data types	sp_addtype sp_droptype	CREATE TYPE DROP TYPE	sp_addtype sp_droptype
Data types	**timestamp** syntax for **rowversion** data type	**rowversion** data type syntax	TIMESTAMP
Data types	Ability to insert null values into **timestamp** columns.	Use a DEFAULT instead.	INSERT NULL into TIMESTAMP columns
Data types	'text in row' table option	Use **varchar(max)**, **nvarchar(max)**, and **varbinary(max)**	Text in row table option

		data types. For more information, see sp_tableoption (Transact-SQL).	
Data types	Data types: text ntext image	Use **varchar(max)**, **nvarchar(max)**, and **varbinary(max)** data types.	Data types: **text ntext** or **image**
Database management	**sp_attach_db** **sp_attach_single_file_db**	CREATE DATABASE statement with the FOR ATTACH option. To rebuild multiple log files, when one or more have a new location, use the FOR ATTACH_REBUILD_LOG option.	**sp_attach_db** **sp_attach_single_file_db**
Database objects	CREATE DEFAULT DROP DEFAULT **sp_bindefault** **sp_unbindefault**	DEFAULT keyword in CREATE TABLE and ALTER TABLE	CREATE_DROP_DEFAULT **sp_bindefault** **sp_unbindefault**
Database objects	CREATE RULE DROP RULE **sp_bindrule** **sp_unbindrule**	CHECK keyword in CREATE TABLE and ALTER TABLE	CREATE_DROP_RULE **sp_bindrule** **sp_unbindrule**
Database objects	**sp_depends**	**sys.dm_sql_referencing_entities** and **sys.dm_sql_referenced_entities**	**sp_depends**
Database objects	**sp_renamedb**	MODIFY NAME in ALTER DATABASE	**sp_renamedb**

SQL Server Supporting Technology

Database objects	sp_getbindtoken	Use MARS or distributed transactions.	sp_getbindtoken
Database options	sp_bindsession	Use MARS or distributed transactions.	sp_bindsession
Database options	sp_resetstatus	ALTER DATABASE SET { ONLINE | EMERGENCY }	sp_resetstatus
Database options	TORN_PAGE_DETECTION option of ALTER DATABASE	PAGE_VERIFY TORN_PAGE_DETECTION option of ALTER DATABASE	ALTER DATABASE WITH TORN_PAGE_DETECTION
DBCC	DBCC DBREINDEX	REBUILD option of ALTER INDEX.	DBCC DBREINDEX
DBCC	DBCC INDEXDEFRAG	REORGANIZE option of ALTER INDEX	DBCC INDEXDEFRAG
DBCC	DBCC SHOWCONTIG	sys.dm_db_index_physical_stats	DBCC SHOWCONTIG
DBCC	DBCC PINTABLE DBCC UNPINTABLE	Has no effect.	DBCC [UN]PINTABLE
Extended properties	Level0type = 'type' and Level0type = 'USER' to add extended properties to level-1 or level-2 type objects.	Use Level0type = 'USER' only to add an extended property directly to a user or role. Use Level0type = 'SCHEMA' to add an extended property to level-1 types such as TABLE or VIEW, or level-2 types such as COLUMN or TRIGGER. For more information, see sp_addextendedproperty (Transact-SQL).	EXTPROP_LEVEL0TYPE EXTPROP_LEVEL0USER

Extended stored procedure programming	srv_alloc srv_convert srv_describe srv_getbindtoken srv_got_attention srv_message_handler srv_paramdata srv_paraminfo srv_paramlen srv_parammaxlen srv_paramname srv_paramnumber srv_paramset srv_paramsetoutput srv_paramtype srv_pfield srv_pfieldex srv_rpcdb srv_rpcname srv_rpcnumber srv_rpcoptions srv_rpcowner srv_rpcparams srv_senddone srv_sendmsg srv_sendrow	Use CLR Integration instead.	XP_API

SQL Server Supporting Technology

	srv_setcoldata		
	srv_setcollen		
	srv_setutype		
	srv_willconvert		
	srv_wsendmsg		
Extended stored procedure programming	sp_addextendedproc sp_dropextendedproc sp_helpextendedproc	Use CLR Integration instead.	sp_addextendedproc sp_dropextendedproc sp_helpextendedproc
Extended stored procedures	xp_grantlogin xp_revokelogin xp_loginConfig	• Use CREATE LOGIN • Use DROP LOGIN **IsIntegratedSecurityOnly** argument of SERVERPROPERTY	xp_grantlogin xp_revokelogin xp_loginconfig
Full-text search	CREATE FULLTEXT CATALOG option: IN PATH '*rootpath*'	None.	
Full-text search	DATABASEPROPERTYEX property: **IsFullTextEnabled**	None.	DATABASEPROPERTYEX(**'IsFullTextEnabled'**)
Full-text search	FULLTEXTCATALOGPROPERTY property: **LogSize** **PopulateStatus**	None.	FULLTEXTCATALOGPROPERTY(**'LogSize'**) FULLTEXTCATALOGPROPERTY(**'PopulateStatus'**)
Full-text	FULLTEXTSERVICEPROPERTY property:	None.	FULLTEXTSERVICEPROPERTY(**'ConnectTimeout'**)

SQL Server Supporting Technology

search	ConnectTimeout		FULLTEXTSERVICEPROPERTY('DataTimeout')
	DataTimeout		FULLTEXTSERVICEPROPERTY('ResourceUsage')
	ResourceUsage		
Full-text search	sp_configure options: ft crawl bandwidth ft notify bandwidth	None.	sp_configure 'ft crawl bandwidth (max)' sp_configure 'ft crawl bandwidth (min)' sp_configure 'ft notify bandwidth (max)' sp_configure 'ft notify bandwidth (min)'
Full-text search	sp_detach_db option: [@keepfulltextindexfile =] 'KeepFulltextIndexFile'	None.	sp_detach_db @keepfulltextindexfile
Full-text search	sp_fulltext_catalog	CREATE FULL CATALOG ALTER FULLTEXT CATALOG DROP FULLTEXT CATALOG	sp_fulltext_catalog
Full-text search	sp_fulltext_column sp_fulltext_database sp_fulltext_table	CREATE FULL INDEX ALTER FULLTEXT INDEX DROP FULLTEXT	sp_fulltext_column sp_fulltext_database sp_fulltext_table

SQL Server Supporting Technology

		INDEX	
Full-text search	sp_help_fulltext_catalogs	sys.fulltext_catalogs	sp_help_fulltext_catalogs
	sp_help_fulltext_catalog_components	sys.fulltext_index_columns	sp_help_fulltext_catalog_components
	sp_help_fulltext_catalogs_cursor	sys.fulltext_indexes	sp_help_fulltext_catalogs_cursor
	sp_help_fulltext_columns		sp_help_fulltext_columns
	sp_help_fulltext_columns_cursor		sp_help_fulltext_columns_cursor
	sp_help_fulltext_tables		sp_help_fulltext_table
	sp_help_fulltext_tables_cursor		sp_help_fulltext_tables_cursor
Full-text search	sp_fulltext_service action values: **clean_up, connect_timeout,** and **data_timeout** return zero **resource_usage** has no function.	None	**sp_fulltext_service** @action=clean_up **sp_fulltext_service** @action=connect_timeout **sp_fulltext_service** @action=data_timeout **sp_fulltext_service** @action=resource_usage
Full-text	sys.dm_fts_active_catalogs columns:	None.	dm_fts_active_catalogs.is_paused

search	is_paused		dm_fts_active_catalogs.previous_status
	previous_status		dm_fts_active_catalogs.previous_status_description
	previous_status_description		
	row_count_in_thousands		dm_fts_active_catalogs.row_count_in_thousands
	status		dm_fts_active_catalogs.status
	status_description		
	worker_count		dm_fts_active_catalogs.status_description
			dm_fts_active_catalogs.worker_count
Full-text search	sys.dm_fts_memory_buffers column: row_count	None.	dm_fts_memory_buffers.row_count
Full-text search	sys.fulltext_catalogs columns: path data_space_id file_id columns	None.	fulltext_catalogs.path fulltext_catalogs.data_space_id fulltext_catalogs.file_id
Functions	fn_get_sql	sys.dm_exec_sql_text	fn_get_sql
Index options	sp_indexoption	ALTER INDEX	sp_indexoption
Index options	CREATE TABLE, ALTER TABLE, or CREATE INDEX syntax without	Rewrite the statement to use the current syntax.	INDEX_OPTION

SQL Server Supporting Technology

	parentheses around the options.		
Database objects	Ability to return result sets from triggers	None	Returning results from trigger
Instance options	sp_configure options: 'allow updates'	System tables are no longer updatable. Setting has no effect.	sp_configure 'allow updates'
Instance options	sp_configure options: 'locks' 'open objects' 'set working set size'	Now automatically configured. Setting has no effect.	sp_configure 'locks' sp_configure 'open objects' sp_configure 'set working set size'
Instance option	sp_configure options: 'user instances enabled'	No longer needed as SQL Server Compact 3.5 SP1 provides the necessary functionality. Setting has no effect.	None
Instance option	sp_configure options: 'priority boost'	System tables are no longer updatable. Setting has no effect.	sp_configure 'priority boost'
Instance option	sp_configure options: 'remote proc trans'	System tables are no longer updatable. Setting has no effect.	sp_configure 'remote proc trans'
Locking	sp_lock	Query sys.dm_tran_locks	sp_lock
Metadata	FILE_ID INDEXKEY_PROPERTY	FILE_IDEX sys.index_columns	FILE_ID INDEXKEY_PROPERTY
Progra	SQL Server Database	SQL Server	SQL Server Database

mmab ility	Management Objects (SQL-DMO)	Management Objects (SMO)	Management Objects (SQL-DMO) has been removed from SQL Server 2008 Express Edition and will be removed from other editions. We recommend that you modify applications that currently use this feature as soon as possible. If you must support SQL-DMO for SQL Server Express, install the Backward Compatibility Components from the SQL Server 2005 feature pack from the Microsoft Download Center. Do not use SQL-DMO in new development work; use SQL Server Management Objects (SMO) instead. You can obtain the SMO documentation by installing SQL Server 2005 Books Online.
Removable databases	sp_certify_removable sp_create_removable	sp_detach_db	sp_certify_removable sp_create_removable
Removable databases	sp_dbremove	DROP DATABASE	sp_dbremove
Security	The ALTER LOGIN WITH SET CREDENTIAL syntax	Replaced by the new ALTER LOGIN ADD and DROP CREDENTIAL syntax	ALTER LOGIN WITH SET CREDENTIAL
Security	sp_addapprole sp_dropapprole	• CREATE APPLICATION ROLE • DROP APPLICATION ROLE	sp_addapprole sp_dropapprole

Security	sp_addlogin	• CREATE LOGIN	sp_addlogin
	sp_droplogin	• DROP LOGIN	sp_droplogin
Security	sp_adduser	CREATE USER	sp_adduser
	sp_dropuser	DROP USER	sp_dropuser
Security	sp_grantdbaccess	CREATE USER	sp_grantdbaccess
	sp_revokedbaccess	DROP USER	sp_revokedbaccess
Security	sp_addrole	CREATE ROLE	sp_addrole
	sp_droprole	DROP ROLE	sp_droprole
Security	sp_approlepassword	ALTER APPLICATION ROLE	sp_approlepassword
	sp_password	ALTER LOGIN	sp_password
Security	sp_changeobjectowner	ALTER SCHEMA or ALTER AUTHORIZATION	sp_changeobjectowner
Security	sp_defaultdb sp_defaultlanguage	ALTER LOGIN	sp_defaultdb
			sp_defaultlanguage
Security	sp_denylogin sp_grantlogin	ALTER LOGIN DISABLE	sp_denylogin
	sp_revokelogin	CREATE LOGIN	sp_grantlogin
		DROP LOGIN	sp_revokelogin
Security	USER_ID	DATABASE_PRINCIPAL_ID	USER_ID
Security	sp_srvrolepermission	These stored procedures return information that	sp_srvrolepermission

	sp_dbfixedrolepermission	was correct in SQL Server 2000. The output does not reflect changes to the permissions hierarchy implemented in SQL Server 2008. For more information, see Permissions of Fixed Server Roles (Database Engine).	**sp_dbfixedrolepermission**
Security	GRANT ALL DENY ALL REVOKE ALL	GRANT, DENY, and REVOKE specific permissions.	ALL Permission
Security	PERMISSIONS intrinsic function	Query **sys.fn_my_permissions** instead.	PERMISSIONS
Security	SETUSER	EXECUTE AS	SETUSER
SET options	SET ANSI_NULLS SET ANSI_PADDING SET CONCAT_NULL_YIELDS_NULL SET OFFSETS	None	SET ANSI_NULLS OFF SET ANSI_PADDING OFF SET CONCAT_NULL_YIELDS_ NULL OFF SET OFFSETS
System tables	**sysaltfiles** **syscacheobjects** **syscolumns**	Compatibility views. For more information, see Compatibility Views (Transact-SQL).	**sysaltfiles** **syscacheobjects** **syscharsets**

SQL Server Supporting Technology

syscomments	✏️**Important:**	syscolumns
sysconfigures		syscomments
sysconstraints	The compatibility views do not expose metadata for features that were introduced in SQL Server 2005. We recommend that you upgrade your applications to use catalog views. For more information, see Catalog Views (Transact-SQL).	sysconfigures
syscurconfigs		sysconstraints
sysdatabases		sysconstraints
sysdepends		sysdatabases
sysdevices		sysdepends
sysfilegroups		sysdevices
sysfiles		sysfilegroups
sysforeignkeys		sysfiles
sysfulltextcatalogs		sysforeignkeys
sysindexes		sysfulltextcatalogs
sysindexkeys		sysindexes
syslockinfo		sysindexkeys
syslogins		syslanguages
sysmembers		syslockinfo
sysmessages		syslogins
sysobjects		sysmembers
sysoledbusers		sysmessages
sysopentapes		sysobjects

SQL Server Supporting Technology

	sysperfinfo		sysoledbusers
	syspermissions		sysopentapes
	sysprocesses		sysperfinfo
	sysprotects		syspermissions
	sysreferences		sysprocesses
	sysremotelogins		sysprotects
	sysservers		sysreferences
	systypes		sysremotelogins
	sysusers		sysservers
			systypes
			sysusers
System tables	sys.numbered_procedures sys.numbered_procedure_parameters	None	numbered_procedures numbered_procedure_parameters
System functions	fn_virtualservernodes fn_servershareddrives	Select from dm_os_cluster_nodes and sys.dm_io_cluster_shared_drives.	fn_virtualservernodes fn_servershareddrives
System views	sys.sql_dependencies	sys.sql_expression_dependencies	sys.sql_dependencies
Table compression	The use of the vardecimal storage format.	Vardecimal storage format is deprecated. SQL Server 2008 data compression compresses decimal values as well as	Vardecimal storage format

SQL Server Supporting Technology

		other data types. We recommend that you use data compression instead of the vardecimal storage format.	
Table compression	Use of the **sp_db_vardecimal _storage_format** procedure.	Vardecimal storage format is deprecated. SQL Server 2008 data compression compresses decimal values as well as other data types. We recommend that you use data compression instead of the vardecimal storage format.	**sp_db_vardecimal_storage_format**
Table compression	Use of the **sp_estimated_rowsize_reduction_for_vardecimal** procedure.	Use data compression and the sp_estimate_data_compression_savings procedure instead.	**sp_estimated_rowsize_reduction_for_vardecimal**
Table hints	Specifying NOLOCK or READUNCOMMITTED in the FROM clause of an UPDATE or DELETE statement.	Remove the NOLOCK or READUNCOMMITTED table hints from the FROM clause.	NOLOCK or READUNCOMMITTED in UPDATE or DELETE
Table hints	Specifying table hints without using the WITH keyword.	Use WITH.	Table hint without **WITH**
Table hints			HOLDLOCK table hint without parenthesis
Table hints			INSERT_HINTS
Textpointers	WRITETEXT UPDATETEXT READTEXT	None	UPDATETEXT or WRITETEXT READTEXT
Textpointer	TEXTPTR()	None	TEXTPTR

SQL Server Supporting Technology

s		TEXTVALID()	TEXTVALID
Transact-SQL	:: function-calling sequence	Replaced by SELECT column_list FROM sys.<function_name>(). For example, replace SELECT * FROM ::fn_virtualfilestats(2, 1) with SELECT * FROM sys.fn_virtualfilestats(2,1).	'::' function calling syntax
Transact-SQL	Three-part and four-part column references in SELECT list	Two-part names is the standard-compliant behavior.	More than two-part column name
Transact-SQL	A string enclosed in quotation marks used as a column alias for an expression in a SELECT list: 'string_alias' = expression	expression [AS] column_alias expression [AS] [column_alias] expression [AS] "column_alias" expression [AS] 'column_alias' column_alias = expression	String literals as column aliases
Transact-SQL	Numbered procedures	None. Do not use.	ProcNums
Transact-SQL	table_name.index_name syntax in DROP INDEX	index_name ON table_name syntax in DROP INDEX.	DROP INDEX with two-part name
Transact-SQL	Not ending Transact-SQL statements with a semicolon.	End Transact-SQL statements with a semicolon (;).	None
Transact-SQL	GROUP BY ALL	Use custom case-by-case solution with UNION or derived table.	GROUP BY ALL
Trans	ROWGUIDCOL as a	Use $rowguid.	ROWGUIDCOL

Transact-SQL	column name in DML statements.		
Transact-SQL	IDENTITYCOL as a column name in DML statements.	Use $identity.	IDENTITYCOL
Transact-SQL	Use of #, ## as temporary table and temporary stored procedure names.	Use at least one additional character.	'#' and '##' as the name of temporary tables and stored procedures
Transact-SQL	Use of @, @@, or @@ as Transact-SQL identifiers.	Do not use @ or @@ or names that begin with @@ as identifiers.	'@' and names that start with '@@' as Transact-SQL identifiers
Transact-SQL	Use of DEFAULT keyword as default value.	Do not use the word DEFAULT as a default value.	DEFAULT keyword as a default value
Transact-SQL	Use of a space as a separator between table hints.	Use a comma to separate table hints.	Multiple table hints without comma
Transact-SQL	The select list of an aggregate indexed view must contain COUNT_BIG (*) in 90 compatibility mode	Use COUNT_BIG (*).	Index view select list without COUNT_BIG(*)
Transact-SQL	The indirect application of table hints to an invocation of a multi-statement table-valued function (TVF) through a view.	None.	Indirect TVF hints
Transact-SQL	ALTER DATABASE syntax: MODIFY FILEGROUP READONLY MODIFY FILEGROUP	• Use READ_ONLY instead. • Use READ_WRITE instead.	MODIFY FILEGROUP READONLY MODIFY FILEGROUP READWRITE

	READWRITE	
Linked servers	A linked server uses OLEDB.	Using OLEDB for linked servers

SQL Server Supporting Technology

Deprecated Database Engine Features in SQL Server 2005

February 2007

Deprecated features include features that will not be supported in the next version of SQL Server and features that will not be supported in a future version of SQL Server.

These Database Engine features will not be supported in the next version of SQL Server. We recommend that, as time allows, you replace these features with the replacement item if possible.

Category	Deprecated feature	Replacement
Backup and restore	DUMP statement	BACKUP
Backup and restore	LOAD statement	RESTORE
Backup and restore	BACKUP LOG WITH NO_LOG	None. The transaction log is automatically truncated when the database is using the simple recovery model. If you need to remove the log backup chain from a database, switch to the simple recovery model.
Backup and restore	BACKUP LOG WITH TRUNCATE_ONLY	None. The transaction log is automatically truncated when the database is using the simple recovery model. If you need to remove the log backup chain from a database, switch to the simple recovery model.
Backup and restore	BACKUP TRANSACTION	BACKUP LOG
Backup and	BACKUP { DATABASE	LOG } WITH	None.

restore	PASSWORD	
Backup and restore	BACKUP { DATABASE | LOG } WITH MEDIAPASSWORD	None.
Backup and Restore	RESTORE { DATABASE | LOG } ... WITH DBO_ONLY	RESTORE { DATABASE | LOG } ... ... WITH RESTRICTED_USER
Backup and restore	RESTORE { DATABASE | LOG } WITH PASSWORD	None.
Backup and restore	RESTORE { DATABASE | LOG } WITH MEDIAPASSWORD	None.
Compatibility levels	60 and 65 compatibility levels	None.
Compatibility levels	70 compatibility level	None.
DBCC	DBCC CONCURRENCYVIOLATION	None.
Extended stored procedure programming	**srv_getuserdata** **srv_setuserdata**	Use CLR Integration instead.
Full-text search	**sp_fulltext_service** action values **clean_up**, **connect_timeout**, and **data_timeout** return zero.	None.
Instance options	SET REMOTE_PROC_TRANSACTIONS **sp_configure** *'remote proc trans'*	Use linked servers and distributed queries. **sp_addlinkedserver**
Remote servers	Use of remote servers **sp_addserver** to create remote servers	Use linked servers. **sp_addlinkedserver** to create linked servers
Security	**sp_addalias** **sp_dropalias** **sp_addgroup** **sp_changegroup** **sp_dropgroup** **sp_helpgroup**	Superseded by roles
Security	**SETUSER**	EXECUTE AS

SQL Server Supporting Technology

| System tables | syssegments | None. |

These Database Engine features are supported in the next version of SQL Server, but will be removed in a later version. The specific version of SQL Server has not been determined.

Category	Deprecated feature	Replacement
Backup and restore	sp_helpdevice	sys.backup_devices
Collations	Hindi Lithuanian_Classic SQL_AltDiction_CP1253_CS_AS	None. These collations exist in Microsoft SQL Server 2005, but are not visible through **fn_helpcollations**.
Compatibility level	80 compatibility level	None. For more information about compatibility levels, see sp_dbcmptlevel (Transact-SQL).
Data types	sp_addtype	CREATE TYPE
Data types	**timestamp** syntax for **rowversion** data type	**rowversion** data type syntax.
Database management	sp_attach_db sp_attach_single_file_db	CREATE DATABASE statement with the FOR ATTACH option; to rebuild multiple log files, when one or more have a new location, use the FOR ATTACH_REBUILD_LOG option.
Database objects	CREATE DEFAULT DROP DEFAULT **sp_bindefault** **sp_unbindefault**	DEFAULT keyword in CREATE/ALTER TABLE.
Database objects	CREATE RULE DROP RULE **sp_bindrule** **sp_unbindrule**	CHECK keyword in CREATE/ALTER TABLE.
Database objects	sp_renamedb	MODIFY NAME in ALTER DATABASE.
Database	Ability to return result sets from triggers	None.

	objects		
Database options	'concat null yields null' of **sp_dboption**	None.	
Database options	**sp_dboption** **sp_resetstatus**	ALTER DATABASE SET { ONLINE | EMERGENCY }	
Database options	TORN_PAGE_DETECTION option of ALTER DATABASE	PAGE_VERIFY TORN_PAGE DETECTION option of ALTER DATABASE	
DBCC	DBCC DBREINDEX	REBUILD option of ALTER INDEX.	
DBCC	DBCC INDEXDEFRAG	REORGANIZE option of ALTER INDEX	
DBCC	DBCC SHOWCONTIG	**sys.dm_db_index_physical_stats**	
Extended properties	Level0type = 'type' and Level0type = 'USER' to add extended properties to level-1 or level-2 type objects.	Use **Level0type** = 'USER' only to add an extended property directly to a user or role. Use **Level0type** = 'SCHEMA' to add an extended property to level-1 types like TABLE or VIEW, or level-2 types like COLUMN or TRIGGER. For more information, see sp_addextendedproperty (Transact-SQL).	
Extended stored procedure programming	srv_alloc srv_convert srv_describe srv_getbindtoken srv_got_attention srv_message_handler srv_paramdata srv_paraminfo srv_paramlen srv_parammaxlen srv_paramname srv_paramnumber	Use CLR Integration instead.	

SQL Server Supporting Technology

	srv_paramset		
	srv_paramsetoutput		
	srv_paramtype		
	srv_pfield		
	srv_pfieldex		
	srv_rpcdb		
	srv_rpcname		
	srv_rpcnumber		
	srv_rpcoptions		
	srv_rpcowner		
	srv_rpcparams		
	srv_senddone		
	srv_sendmsg		
	srv_sendrow		
	srv_setcoldata		
	srv_setcollen		
	srv_setutype		
	srv_willconvert		
	srv_wsendmsg		
Extended stored procedure programming	sp_addextendedproc sp_dropextendedproc sp_helpextendedproc	Use CLR Integration instead.	
Extended stored procedures	xp_LoginConfig	**IsIntegratedSecurityOnly** argument of SERVERPROPERTY	
Full-text search	sp_fulltext_catalog	CREATE/ALTER/DROP CATALOG	FULLTEXT
Full-text	sp_fulltext_table	CREATE/ALTER/DROP INDEX	FULLTEXT

SQL Server Supporting Technology

search	**sp_fulltext_column**	ALTER FULLTEXT INDEX
	sp_fulltext_database	
Full-text search	**sp_help_fulltext_tables**[**_cursor**] **sp_help_fulltext_columns**[**_cursor**]	**sys.fulltext_indexes** **sys.fulltext_index_columns**
	sp_help_fulltext_catalogs[**_cursor**]	**sys.fulltext_catalogs**
Functions	**fn_get_sql**	**sys.dm_exec_sql_text**
Index options	**sp_indexoption** **fillfactor = 0**	ALTER INDEX **fillfactor = 100**
Index options	CREATE INDEX <*index_option*>::= syntax	CREATE INDEX <*relational_index_option*>::= syntax
Instance options	Default setting of **disallow results from triggers** option = 0	Default setting of **disallow results from triggers** option = 1
Locking	**sp_lock**	**sys.syslock_information**
Locking	**syslockinfo**	**sys.syslock_information**
Metadata	DATABASEPROPERTY FILE_ID	DATABASEPROPERTYEX FILE_IDEX
	INDEXKEY_PROPERTY	**sys.index_columns**
Other	DB-Library Embedded SQL for C	Although the SQL Server 2005 Database Engine still supports connections from existing applications using the DB-Library and Embedded SQL APIs, it does not include the files or documentation needed to do programming work on applications that use these APIs. A future version of the SQL Server Database Engine will drop support for connections from DB-Library or Embedded SQL applications. Do not use DB-Library or Embedded SQL to develop new applications. Remove any dependencies on either DB-Library or Embedded SQL when modifying existing applications. Instead of these APIs, use the SQLClient namespace or an API such as OLE DB or ODBC. SQL Server 2005 does not include the DB-Library DLL required to run these applications. To run DB-Library or Embedded SQL applications you must

SQL Server Supporting Technology

		have available the DB-Library DLL from SQL Server version 6.5, SQL Server 7.0, or SQL Server 2000.
Query hints	FASTFIRSTROW hint	OPTION (FAST n).
Removable databases	**sp_certify_removable** **sp_create_removable**	sp_detach_db
Removable databases	**sp_dbremove**	DROP DATABASE
Security	**sp_addapprole** **sp_dropapprole**	CREATE APPLICATION ROLE DROP APPLICATION ROLE
Security	**sp_addlogin** **sp_droplogin**	CREATE LOGIN DROP LOGIN
Security	**sp_adduser** **sp_dropuser**	CREATE USER DROP USER
Security	**sp_grantdbaccess** **sp_revokedbaccess**	CREATE USER DROP USER
Security	**sp_addrole** **sp_droprole**	CREATE ROLE DROP ROLE
Security	**sp_approlepassword** **sp_password**	ALTER APPLICATION ROLE ALTER LOGIN
Security	**sp_changeobjectowner**	ALTER SCHEMA or ALTER AUTHORIZATION
Security	**sp_defaultdb** **sp_defaultlanguage**	ALTER LOGIN
Security	**sp_denylogin** **sp_grantlogin**	ALTER LOGIN DISABLE CREATE LOGIN
	sp_revokelogin	DROP LOGIN
Security	USER_ID FILE_ID	DATABASE_PRINCIPAL_ID FILE_IDEX
Security	**sp_srvrolepermission** **sp_dbfixedrolepermission**	These stored procedures return information that was correct in SQL Server 2000. The output does not reflect changes to the permissions hierarchy implemented in SQL Server 2005. For more information, see "Permissions of Fixed Roles" in SQL Server 2005 Books Online.

SQL Server Supporting Technology

SET options	SET ANSI_NULLS SET ANSI_PADDING SET CONCAT_NULL_YIELDS_NULL	None.
SET options	SET OFFSETS	None.
SET options	SET ROWCOUNT for INSERT, UPDATE, and DELETE statements	TOP keyword.
System tables	sysaltfiles syscacheobjects syscolumns syscomments sysconfigures sysconstraints syscurconfigs sysdatabases sysdepends sysdevices sysfilegroups sysfiles sysforeignkeys sysfulltextcatalogs sysindexes sysindexkeys syslockinfo syslogins sysmembers sysmessages sysobjects sysoledbusers	Compatibility views. For more information, see Compatibility Views (Transact-SQL). **⚠Important:** The compatibility views do not expose metadata for features introduced in SQL Server 2005. It is recommended that you upgrade your applications to use catalog views. For more information, see Catalog Views (Transact-SQL).

SQL Server Supporting Technology

	sysopentapes		
	sysperfinfo		
	syspermissions		
	sysprocesses		
	sysprotects		
	sysreferences		
	sysremotelogins		
	sysservers		
	systypes		
	sysusers		
Table hints	Specifying NOLOCK or READUNCOMMITTED in the FROM clause of an UPDATE or DELETE statement when applied to the target table of the statement.	Remove the NOLOCK or READUNCOMMITTED table hints from the FROM clause.	
Textpointers	READTEXT, WRITETEXT, UPDATETEXT	None.	
Textpointers	'text in row' table option	Use **varchar(max)**, **nvarchar(max)**, and **varbinary(max)** data types. For more information, see sp_tableoption (Transact-SQL).	
Textpointers	TEXT, NTEXT and IMAGE data types	Use **varchar(max)**, **nvarchar(max)**, and **varbinary(max)** data types.	
Textpointers	TEXTPTR(), TEXTVALID()	None.	
Transact-SQL	:: function-calling sequence	Replaced by SELECT *column_list* FROM **sys.fn_function_name()**	
Transact-SQL	3-part and 4-part column references in SELECT list	2-part names is the standard-compliant behavior.	
Transact-SQL	A string enclosed in quotes used as a column alias for an expression in a SELECT list: '*string_alias*' = *expression*	*expression* [AS] *column_alias* *expression* [AS] [*column_alias*] *expression* [AS] "*column_alias*" *expression* [AS] '*column_alias*'	

		column_alias = expression
Transact-SQL	Stored procedure numbers **sys.numbered_procedures** **sys.numbered_procedure_parameters**	None.
Transact-SQL	*table_name.index_name* syntax in DROP INDEX	*index_name* ON *table_name* syntax in DROP INDEX.
Transact-SQL	UPDATE table1, table2, ... SET syntax	Specifying more than one table in the UPDATE target is nonstandard and ambiguous.

Release	History
1 February 2007	**Changed content:** • Removed **syslanguages** and **syscharsets** from the table of features not supported in a future version of SQL Server.
17 July 2006	**New content:** • Added **syssegments** to table of features not supported in next version of SQL Server.

Deprecated Features in SQL Server 2005 Replication

SP1 – January 2006

This topic describes replication features that will be removed in a future release. The features are available in Microsoft SQL Server 2005, but we recommend that you use alternative features when possible.

The following features, which apply to all types of replication, have been deprecated in SQL Server 2005.

Feature	Description
Attachable subscriptions	This feature can be used when deploying a large number of pull subscriptions, which is common in merge replication. In SQL Server 2005, we recommend that you use the following approaches rather than attachable subscriptions: • For merge publications that are partitioned using parameterized filters, we recommend that you use the new features of partitioned snapshots, which simplify the initialization of a large number of subscriptions. For more information, see Snapshots for Merge Publications with Parameterized Filters. • For publications that are not partitioned, you can initialize a subscription with a backup. For more information, see Initializing a Merge Subscription Without a Snapshot and Initializing a Transactional Subscription Without a Snapshot. In both cases, you can automate the creation of a large number of subscriptions with scripting: create a single subscription; script it; modify the script for each Subscriber; and apply the script at each Subscriber to create a subscription. For more information, see Scripting Replication. For more information about attachable subscriptions, see Attachable Subscriptions.
Subscriber registration	The stored procedure sp_addsubscriber (Transact-SQL) is deprecated. It is no longer required to explicitly register a Subscriber at the

SQL Server Supporting Technology

	Publisher.
SQL Distributed Management Objects (SQL-DMO)	Existing code will continue to work, but SQL-DMO does not support new features in SQL Server 2005. Use Replication Management Objects (RMO) instead. For more information, see Programming with Replication Management Objects.
Schema changes using sp_repladdcolumn and sp_repldropcolumn	The stored procedures sp_repladdcolumn (Transact-SQL) and sp_repldropcolumn (Transact-SQL) have been deprecated. Use schema change replication instead. For more information, see Making Schema Changes on Publication Databases. The stored procedures cannot be used for adding or dropping columns with data types introduced in SQL Server 2005: XML, varchar(max), nvarchar(max), varbinary(max), or user defined types (UDT).
Checksum validation	Checksum validation should only be used for Subscribers running Microsoft SQL Server version 7.0. Use binary checksum validation for SQL Server Subscribers running more recent versions. You can also use row count validation for all SQL Server Subscribers, including version 7.0 and those subscribing to publications from Oracle Publishers. For more information, see Validating Replicated Data.
Adding publications to Active Directory	Adding a publication to Active Directory using the @add_to_active_directory parameter of sp_addpublication (Transact-SQL) or sp_addmergepublication (Transact-SQL), has been deprecated. Subscribing to a publication by locating it in Active Directory has been discontinued.
-UseInprocLoader parameter	This parameter of the Distribution Agent and Merge Agent is deprecated because it is not compatible with the XML data type. If you are not replicating XML data, this parameter can be used. For more information, see Replication Distribution Agent and Replication Merge Agent.

The following transactional replication features have been deprecated for SQL Server 2005.

Feature	Description
Subscription expiration for transactional publications	The @retention property of sp_addpublication (Transact-SQL) has been deprecated. Subscriptions are still marked as inactive and must be reinitialized if they have not synchronized within the maximum distribution retention period (the @max_distretention property of sp_adddistributiondb (Transact-SQL). For more information about retention periods, see Subscription Expiration and Deactivation.
"No sync" subscriptions to transactional publications	A subscription is a "no sync" subscription if a value of **none** is specified for the @sync_type parameter of sp_addsubscription (Transact-SQL) parameter. If you want to specify that the necessary schema and data are already present in the subscription database, specify a value of **replication**

SQL Server Supporting Technology

	support only for the parameter instead. For more information, see Initializing a Transactional Subscription Without a Snapshot.
ODBC Subscribers	Use OLE-DB for non-SQL Server Subscribers instead. For information about supported Subscribers, see Non-SQL Server Subscribers.
Transformable subscriptions	This feature is available through the stored procedure interface, but support for this feature in the user interface has been dropped. Using the feature requires installation of Microsoft SQL Server 2000 Data Transformation Services (DTS). For more information, see SQL Server 2005 Integration Services Backward Compatibility. For more information about transformable subscriptions, see Transforming Published Data.
Updatable subscriptions with snapshot publications	Using updatable subscriptions with transactional publications is still supported. For more information, see Updatable Subscriptions for Transactional Replication.
Distribution ActiveX control	This control allows you to embed the Distribution Agent in applications. Use RMO instead. For more information, see Synchronizing Subscriptions (RMO Programming).
Replication Distributor Interface	In SQL Server 2000, the Replication Distributor Interface provided an interface to store replicated transactions in the distribution database on the Distributor. This interface could be used to enable publishing from a non-SQL Server database (additional custom programming was required to track changes on the Publisher). Support for this feature has been deprecated, but existing code will continue to work on a server upgraded from SQL Server 2000. For more information, see "Replication Distributor Interface Reference" in SQL Server 2000 Books Online. SQL Server 2005 supports publishing from Oracle databases without custom programming. For more information, see Oracle Publishing Overview.

The following merge replication features have been deprecated for SQL Server 2005.

Feature	Description
Alternate synchronization partners	The alternate synchronization partners feature allows you to specify an alternate Publisher with which a Subscriber can synchronize. For more information, see Alternate Synchronization Partners. In SQL Server 2005, we recommend that you use merge replication in conjunction with database mirroring, rather than alternate synchronization partners. For more information, see Replication and Database Mirroring.
Merge ActiveX control	This control allows you to embed the Merge Agent in applications. Use RMO instead. For more information, see Synchronizing Subscriptions (RMO Programming).
Multicolumn	When merge replication performs an update, it updates all changed columns in one UPDATE statement and resets unchanged columns to their original

UPDATE option	values. Alternatively, it can issue multiple UPDATE statements, with one UPDATE statement for each column that has changed. The multicolumn UPDATE statement is typically more efficient. In previous versions of SQL Server, it was recommended to specify a value of **false** for the **fast_multicol_updateproc** article option to address cases in which a multicolumn update (one UPDATE statement) might be less efficient: • Most updates involve a small number of columns. • Index maintenance on unchanged columns is high because those columns are reset when updates occur. Due to performance improvements in SQL Server, this option is no longer required for these cases.

Discontinued Functionality in SQL Server 2005 Replication

April 14, 2006

This topic describes replication features that have been discontinued in Microsoft SQL Server 2005. The following replication features have been discontinued in SQL Server 2005.

Feature	Description
Creating push subscriptions without a connection to the Subscriber in the New Subscription Wizard	Creating push subscriptions in the New Subscription Wizard now requires an active connection to the Subscriber during configuration. For more information about using the wizard, see How to: Create a Push Subscription (SQL Server Management Studio).
Using file transfer protocol (FTP) to initialize Subscribers running SQL Server version 7.0	This feature is available for Subscribers running SQL Server 2000 or later versions. For more information, see Transferring Snapshots Through FTP.
Creating subscriptions in Windows Synchronization Manager	You can no longer create subscriptions in Synchronization Manager, but you can still synchronize subscriptions. For more information, see Windows Synchronization Manager.
Subscribing to a publication by locating it in Active Directory	Adding a publication to Active Directory using the @add_to_active_directory parameter of sp_addpublication (Transact-SQL) or sp_addmergepublication (Transact-SQL), has been deprecated. Subscribing to a publication by locating it in Active Directory has been discontinued.
Snapshot ActiveX control	This control allows you to embed the Snapshot Agent in applications. Use the new managed Snapshot Agent instead. For more information, see SnapshotGenerationAgent and How to: Create the Initial Snapshot (RMO Programming).
Remote agent activation	SQL Server 2000 supported running the Distribution Agent or Merge Agent on another computer and then activating that agent remotely using DCOM. Support has been discontinued for Distributors running SQL Server 2005 and later; it has been deprecated for Distributors running earlier versions of SQL Server. For more information, see

SQL Server Supporting Technology

"Remote Agent Activation" in SQL Server 2000 Books Online.

Microsoft Access (Jet 4.0) Subscribers	Jet is the underlying database used by Access, and replication supported subscriptions to Jet databases in SQL Server 2000. These subscriptions are no longer supported. We recommend using Microsoft SQL Server 2005 Express Edition instead. Access can use a SQL Server database as a backend, and SQL Server databases are not affected by this issue. For more information, see Replicating Data to SQL Server Express.

The following transactional replication features have been discontinued in SQL Server 2005.

Feature	Description
Message Queuing option for queued updating subscriptions	With queued updating subscriptions, changes from Subscribers are written to a queue; changes are then read from the queue and delivered to the Publisher by the Queue Reader Agent. In SQL Server 2000, subscriptions could use a SQL Server queue or Message Queuing to queue changes. The type of queue was specified with the **@queue_type** parameter of sp_addpublication (Transact-SQL), which allowed values of **sql** and **msmq** (Message Queuing). In SQL Server 2005, only a value of **sql** is allowed. Existing publications that use Message Queuing are modified during upgrade to use a SQL Server queue. If you have applications that depend on queued updating using Message Queuing, these applications will need to be rewritten to accommodate a SQL Server queue. For more information about queued updating subscriptions, see Updatable Subscriptions for Transactional Replication.

The following merge replication features have been discontinued in SQL Server 2005.

Feature	Description
Publishing from SQL Server 2005 Express Edition	SQL Server MSDE could serve as a Publisher for merge publications. SQL Server Express, the replacement for MSDE, cannot serve as a Publisher. It can subscribe to merge, transactional, and snapshot publications. Merge replication, and transactional replication with updating subscriptions, both allow changes to be propagated from Subscribers back to the Publisher. For more information about replicating to SQL Server Express, see Replicating Data to SQL Server Express.
IVBCustomResolver interface	This interface allowed you to write COM-based custom conflict resolvers in Visual Basic. In SQL Server 2005, we recommend using Business Logic Handlers rather than COM-based resolvers. For more information, see Executing Business Logic During Merge Synchronization. You can still write COM-based resolvers in C++. For more information,

SQL Server Supporting Technology

see COM-Based Custom Resolvers.

SQL Server Supporting Technology

SQL Server Supporting Technology

Printed in the United States
220709BV00001B/15/P